Robert Stoddart Robertson

Roster of the Masonic bodies in Allen County, Indiana :

tableau of officers and members, April 1, 1898

Robert Stoddart Robertson

Roster of the Masonic bodies in Allen County, Indiana : tableau of officers and members, April 1, 1898

ISBN/EAN: 9783337306212

Printed in Europe, USA, Canada, Australia, Japan

Cover: Foto ©ninafisch / pixelio.de

More available books at **www.hansebooks.com**

ROSTER

OF THE

MASONIC BODIES

IN

ALLEN COUNTY,

INDIANA.

TABLEAU OF OFFICERS AND

MEMBERS,

APRIL 1st, 1898.

—

FORT WAYNE.
JOURNAL CO., PRINTERS.
1898.

THE VALLEY OF FORT WAYNE·

AN HISTORICAL ADDRESS, ON MASONRY IN
FORT WAYNE AND ALLEN COUNTY,
INDIANA.

DELIVERED AT THE SCOTTISH RITE BANQUET,
FORT WAYNE, NOVEMBER 25TH, 1897,

BY

ROBERT S. ROBERTSON, 32°.

IN the times of old, when might made right, and when every man looked upon the other as an enemy until friendship were proven, Masons met in the secluded valley, or upon the heights, in the one case to escape observation, in the other to observe, and thus be free from the spyings of eavesdroppers, and alert to ward off the approach of enemies.

Paradox as it may seem, the Masons, dwellers in the Valley of Fort Wayne, occupy the summit of the heights, for we are at the summit of the water flow to the Gulf of St. Lawrence, and to the Gulf of Mexico, and at the same time are in a basin as we go towards the poles. In other words, do we travel east or west, we descend from the summit. Do we travel north or south we must ascend out of the valley and climb the heights, so that we fulfill the ancient precepts, by locating our lodge at once in the valley, and upon the mountain top.

The history of Masonry in Fort Wayne is almost, if not quite, coeval with the history of the place itself. To be sure, long years passed after adventurous footsteps of the whites had trodden a path to and from the Indian Village of Ke-ki-on-ga, before any thing like a permanent settlement had been made at the meeting of our waters. Years which were full of adventure, of scalpings and burnings, of torture by fire, and torture by captivity and degradation, while the masters of the region were the savage redmen; but no sooner did the first lappings of the wave of civilization ripple and break over its sands, than with it came the precepts, the teachings, and the practice, of Ancient and Accepted Free Masonry.

The warwhoop had scarcely ceased resounding, the red man was still here, the wolf was still howling about the settler's cabin, when a little band of brethren, faithful to the teachings of mother lodge, but far away from its shelter, met and organized a lodge in the wilderness, at the summit of the parting waters of the Maumee and the Wabash, in the Valley of Fort Wayne.

In 1823, when but a little cluster of cabins nestled near the fort so lately abandoned by its military occupants; when northward there was not a white man's house to the Michigan line, and none between Fort Wayne and Chicago, which itself was but a fort and Indian trading post, of no more note than was Fort Wayne; when perhaps not one hundred voters lived in all that is now the County of Allen; when there was no newspaper within one hundred miles; when the state was only seven years old; when Indiana Territory had been organized but twenty-three years; and a year before the County was organized; this little group of the faithful petitioned the Grand Lodge, itself scarcely out of infancy, and located at Madison, on the Ohio, for a charter and dispensation for Masonic work.

On the 22nd of March, 1823, John Sheets, Grand Master of Indiana, granted a dispensation to Alexander Ewing, Worshipful Master; John P. Hedges, Senior Warden, and Benjamin Cushman, Junior Warden, together with all such brethren as might thereafter become members, to form a lodge to be known as "Wayne Lodge of Fort Wayne, County of Randolph, Indiana." Alexander Ewing was a revolutionary officer, the keeper of a tavern on the southwest corner of what are now Barr and Columbia streets, progenitor of a family of much note in all this region. A great grandson, Geo. W. Ewing, III, is a member of Wayne Lodge, and has just become a member of the Lodge of Perfection and Darius Council. John P. Hedges had been an employe of the commissary department, while the fort was garrisoned. Benjamin Cushman was soon after elected one of the first Associate Judges of the Circuit Court.

General John Tipton, a hero of the Indian wars and of Tippecanoe, a United States senator from Indiana, and

6

Grand Master of Masons before the close of his remarkable career, was occupying rooms, or a building within the pickets of the abandoned fort, and there was held the first Masonic Lodge in all this region.

At the first lodge meeting, held some time in May, besides those named in the dispensation, there were present as participators, Captain James Hackley and Benjamin B. Kercheval, and as visitors, General John Tipton, of Pisgah Lodge No. 5, of Corydon; Anthony L. Davis, of Franklin Lodge No. 28, of Kentucky; Richard L. Britton, of St. Johns Lodge No. 13, of Ohio; John McCorkle, one of the proprietors of the town plat of Fort Wayne, of Lodge No. 14, of Ohio; and Robert A. Forsyth, a paymaster in the United States army.

The lodge was opened in Ancient form on the first degree, with Alexander Ewing, W. M., John P. Hedges, S. W. and secretary pro tem, B. Cushman, J. W., James Hackley, treasurer, and B. B. Kercheval, Steward and Tyler pro tem.

Their next meeting was on the 6th of June, when Kercheval was appointed treasurer, Charles W. Ewing, secretary; Jas. Hackley, S. D.; Robert Hars, J. D., and W. Hedges, steward and tyler.

Those named above were the charter members.

On the 10th of October of that year a charter was granted, and John Tipton authorized to constitute and form Wayne Lodge No. 25, which duty he performed November 17th, he joining by demit. The officers installed were:

Alexander Ewing, W. M.; John Tipton, S. W.; B. B. Kercheval, J. W.; Chas. W. Ewing, secretary; A. L. Davis, treasurer; James Hackley, and H. B. McKean, senior and junior deacons, and James Wyman, steward and tyler.

The first election of officers was held December 25th of that year and General Tipton was elected W. M.

The first applicant for degrees was unanimously rejected.

Tipton was re-elected until 1828, and was an efficient officer and worthy member.

Lambert Cushovis was the first to be initiated. August 16, 1824.

The first celebration of St. Johns day was June 24. 1825. when General Tipton delivered the oration. I would give something to see the manuscript, for the brave old fellow scorned the trammels of a spelling book.

The first public installation of officers took place at the house of Hugh Hanna, December 27th, 1825.

The first Masonic burial was that of Capt. Hackley, May 26, 1827. He was a suicide, but the lodge is recorded to have "turned out to gratify Mrs. Hackley."

June 24th, 1827, Alexander Ewing prepared the first Masonic banquet in Fort Wayne, and a few days later the lodge made a loan of fifty dollars to Captain James Riley, the Arabian traveller, author of "Riley's Narrative," proprietor of Willshire, O., and the surveyor of most of the lands about Fort Wayne, to enable him to go east for medical treatment.

The second Masonic funeral was that of the first W. M., Alexander Ewing, January 5, 1828. He died two days before.

Masters were elected as follows:

"Joseph Holman, June 2, 1828,
Lewis G. Thompson, December 1, 1828,
Anthony L. Davis, June 1, 1829,
Hugh Hanna, January 23, 1830,
Absalom Holcomb, June 7, 1830,
Samuel Hanna, June 6, 1831.
Henry Rudisil, February 20, 1833.
Samuel Edsall, June 10, 1833,"

The first by-laws adopted in 1823 provided a fine of 25 cents for the absence of either the W. M., senior and junior wardens, secretary, treasurer, stewards and tyler, and a fine of 12 1-2 cents for deacons and members, unless they presented satisfactory excuse. Any one appearing in the lodge room intoxicated, was to be reprimanded for the first offense, suspended for the second, and expelled for the third. The by-laws numbered sixteen, provided minutely for almost every thing that could properly come before the lodge, and are an evidence of the care and painstaking of the committee which prepared them. After being adopted they were signed by the members present.

After leaving the temporary quarters in the fort, the lodge was held in "Washington hall," on the south west corner of Barr and Columbia. Then a lot was purchased at the northeast corner of Columbia and Harrison, where the Bash block now stands, and a brick lodge room erected, with ante room and preparation, or "goat" room up stairs. This must have been completed about 1831, as on February 7, 1831, a committee reported on the brick work and plastering, but could not tell the "precise" number of brick on account of the snow.

At the June meeting, 1833, a committee reported that they had sold the lot for $1,328.00 to Jos Holman, Richard L. Britton, Francis Comparet, Alex Coquillard and Hugh Hanna. It had been appraised at $1,200.00.

This was because the lodge had suffered, like all others, and ceased to work regularly, on account of the Anti-Masonic excitement growing out of the disappearance of William Morgan in 1826.

On the 20th of February, 1833, the first meeting held since May 7, 1832, the lodge adopted the following resolution.

"Resolved, that whereas, owing to the great excitement prevailing in this section of the country and elsewhere, against the Masonic institutions and Masonry in general, this lodge has not held her regular meetings for seven or eight months past, therefore

Resolved by unanimous consent, that the proceedings shall be as valid and have the same effect as if the same had been done and transacted at the regular meetings of the

9

lodge, and that all by-laws, rules and regulations in any way contravening any of the proceedings of this meeting is hereby suspended."

The lodge was reported on to Grand Lodge in 1833, and 1835 as meeting irregularly, but as the Grand Lodge itself was almost dormant, it took no steps to revoke the charter, or arrest it. The lodge held meetings irregularly, and must have initiated members, the records of which were either never made, or were lost.

It is worthy of note that in those troubled times, when Masons were boycotted in business and ostracised socially, until many were bankrupted and had to seek their fortunes in new fields, one Jared Darrow came to Fort Wayne from western New York, but located on a farm near Roanoke. His coming here was solely on account of the Morgan uprising. He often visited the lodge in Fort Wayne, but it is not known that he became a member. Some time later Stephen Brown Bond came from Lockport, N. Y. for the same reason. He too was a Mason. He married the daughter of Darrow, and two sons, Charles D. and Jared D. Bond were worthy lodge members, and a grandson, and the husbands of two grand daughters are members of our Lodge of Perfection and Council of Princes of Jerusalem. The family has been and is, among our best.

On the 2nd of March, 1840, an earnest attempt was made to reorganize, and the fraternity met at Kiser's hall, on Calhoun street, just south of the alley between Main and Columbia streets, accepted a dispensation and resolved to reorganize as a regular lodge, with Henry Rudisil as W. M.; Simon Edsall, S. W.; Horace B. Taylor, J. W.; Charles E. Sturgis, secretary; T. Daniels and Wm. Rockhill, senior and junior deacons, and A. Holcomb, tyler. They seemed to have labored under the impression that their charter had been revoked, and applied for another, which was granted, but the error was discovered and it continued to work under the old, and the lodge is now the oldest chartered lodge in the state. There seems to be a hiatus in the lodge records from 1833 to 1856, except the record of this one meeting in 1840.

It seemed to work under difficulties until 1847, and the records are wanting, but in that year the charter was declared forfeited for non-payment of dues, and work suspended until July 4th, 1849, when the day was celebrated by a restoration of the charter under date of May 30th, and resumption of Masonic work under Henry Rudisil as Worshipful Master, Samuel Edsall, S. W., and Samuel Shoaff, J. W. The Grand Lodge records of that year show that "The M. W. Grand Master presented a communication from Wayne Lodge No. 25, under suspension for non-payment of dues and failing to be represented, praying the restoration of its charter.

"Which was read, and "on motion by Bro. Kromer,

Referred to the committee on charters and dispensa-8tions." Later appears the following: "26th. Fort Wayne No. 25.—They have examined some letters addressed to the Grand Lodge and individual brethren from Fort Wayne, asking the Grand Lodge to restore the charter of Fort Wayne Lodge No. 25.

The brethren at Fort Wayne have twice forfeited their charter, having had it restored at their request without charge. The present application is too informal in the opinion of your committee, to be granted, especially upon which to restore a forfeited charter. The brethren should apply first for a dispensation, and having thus restored themselves to the confidence of the Grand Lodge, will be entitled to a charter at the next regular communication. They therefore recommend the adoption of the following resolution:

"Resolved, That a dispensation be granted to the brethren at Fort Wayne, when they make application therefor, in proper form."

The petition would seem to have been presented, for later the following appears:

11

"Resolved, That a charter be granted to the petitioners at Fort Wayne, as Fort Wayne Lodge No. 25, and that Henry Rudisill be the W. M., Samuel Edsall, S. W. and S. Shoaff the J. W. of said Lodge, and that the same be without charge to said Lodge."

It will thus be seen that the existence of Wayne Lodge has not been continuous, so far as shown by the records. There is another paragraph in the proceedings of the Grand Lodge, which shows that the charter of Wayne Lodge was at one time stolen and a duplicate was asked and ordered issued.

The old charter is signed by John Sheets, Grand Master; Ex-Governor John Jennings, D. G. M.; Ex-Governor Thomas Posey, S. G. W.; John H. Farnham, Junior G. W., and Wm. C. Keene, secretary.

Before the closing in 1833 the Lodge had 54 members. Of the members prior to 1860, only David F. Comparet, Martin E. Argo, Leopold Falk, Philip Grund and George H. Wilson are believed to be living, and the latter has been treasurer of the Lodge since 1865 continuously.

From Kiser's the Lodge moved to the MacDougal block, thence to the Seidel block, and in 1886 to the Temple. May our Mother Lodge always flourish.

SUMMIT CITY LODGE, No 170.

May 11, 1854, a meeting of Masons was held in Wayne Lodge hall in Kiser's building of which Wm. S. Smith was chairman and Francis S. Aveline was secretary, which resolved to petition the Grand Lodge for a dispensation to form a lodge to be known as Summit City Lodge. The dispensation was granted May 31st, and on the 9th of June a lodge was opened U. D. of which Charles Case was W. M., Francis S. Aveline, S. W. and Yearless Day, J. W.

Sol. D. Bayless W. M., of Wayne Lodge declared Summit City Lodge duly organized U. D. and the first stated meeting was held held June 16, 1854, when the petitions of

12

Warren H. Withers and A. L. Hanna were received. They were the first initiates of the lodge.

June 8, 1855, the first meeting was held under the charter, the charter members being Francis S. Aveline, Charles D. Bond, Charles Case, Yearless Day, David F. Comparet, Charles Hanna, D. W. Maples, Richard W. McMullen, Richard C. Newman and Wm. S. Smith. The lodge was called off till June 18th, when the following officers were elected. Charles Case, W. M.; Francis S. Aveline, S. W.; Wm. S. Smith, J. W., and D. W. Maples, treasurer. Sion S. Bass, a few years later killed in battle as Colonel of the 30th Indiana Vols., Secretary; Henry J. Rudisil, S. D.; Reuben C. F. Rayhouser, J. D.; A. L. Hanna and Charles Hanna, stewards; A. Fisher, tyler, and C. A. Bruce, chaplain. The lodge moved from Kiser's hall to Stewarts, on Calhoun, near Berry, thence to the hall in MacDougal's block in April, 1868, and remained there until removal to the Temple in 1886, their first meeting there being February 26th.

SOL D. BAYLESS LODGE, No. 359,

was instituted June 4th, 13ᵒ.

On the evening of May 4th, 1866, Anson Waring, Martin L. Bulger, John M. Coombs, Byron D. Angell, Alfred Hattersley, Wm. Johnston, Jr., W. Akhurst and Sanford C. Lumbard met in the hall of Wayne Lodge and resolved to petition for a dispensation to form the lodge. The petition was signed by those present and presented to the Grand Lodge at its regular May meeting. By unanimous request of the brethren, Byron D. Angell was appointed W. M., John M. Coombs and Anson Waring were appointed S. W., and J. W. respectively, the dispensation was received and on the 4th of June, those who had petitioned and were named as charter members, met and opened the new lodge in due form.

The first officers elected under the charter were John M. Coombs, W. M.; Anson Waring, S. W.; Wm. Johnston, Jr., J. W. Alfred Hattersley, treasurer; G. W. Durgin, Jr., secre-

13

tary; Chauncey B. Oakley became S. D.; Harry C. Cotter, J. D.; George Esmond, S. S.; John E. Hill, Jr. J. S.; P. O. Blaisdell, tyler.

Its last meeting in the old hall was February 8th, and its first meeting in the Temple February 15th, 1886.

HOME LODGE, No. 342.

A meeting was held at Wayne Lodge hall in the spring of 1868, for the purpose of petitioning for a charter, which was issued July 17th, and the lodge was instituted with the following officers U. D.

Orin D. Hurd, W. M.
Jonathan Knappenberger, S. W.
Martin Cullaton, J. W.
Ferd F. Boltz, S. D.
Milo H. Brooks, J. D.
James E. Graham, Secretary.
Samuel Thanhouser, Treasurer.
John Lillie, Jr., S. S.
Peter Gable, J. S.
S. C. Flutter, Tyler.

The charter was granted May 24th, 1870, and the following were the first officers elected thereafter:

Orin D. Hurd, W. M.
Daniel Gibson, S. W.
Hiram Poyser, J. W.
John Lillie, Secretary.
Samuel Thanhouser, Treasurer
Peter Gable, S. D.
Joseph Wham, J. D.
Christian Boseker, S. S.
Martin V. B. Gotshall, J. S.
James M. Gibson, Tyler.
Robert S. Robertson, Wm H. Brooks and John B. Morgan, trustees.

14

The charter members were as follows:

Orin D. Hurd, Jonathan Knappenberger, Martin Cullaton, Jacob S. Goshorn, James E. Graham, Samuel Thanhouser, Solomon S. Smick, Charles A. Zollinger, Wm. T. Pratt, Gilbert E. Bursley, Ferd F. Boltz, Daniel Gibson, John H. Turner, John W. Hayden, Abram G. Barnett, Milo H. Brooks, Samuel S. Gathley, Wm. Wilmington, Ephraim Stevens, W. A. Roberts, Theodore K. Brackenridge, D. P. Whedon, Robert S. Robertson, John Lillie, Jr., Peter Gable, James W. Ryan, James M. Gibbin, David S. Redelsheimer, John W. Vodermark.

Dispensation was granted July 17, 1868.

The lodge was organized in MacDougal's hall, but moved at once to the hall over the then Post office on Court street, the building now occupied by the Gas Co., and in 1885 moved back to MacDougal's hall, where it remained until it moved into the Temple in 1886.

There have been organized in Allen County, outside of Fort Wayne, the following:

LEO LODGE, No. 224,

AT LEO, ALLEN COUNTY.

Dispensation dated January 10, 1859.

OFFICERS UNDER DISPENSATION.

Edwin L. Knight, W. M.
Jacob Bickhart, S. W.
Kuhnrod Viberg, J. W.

CHARTER MEMBERS.

Edwin L. Knight.   W. M. Dailey.
Harman Viberg.   J. W. Hollopeter.
Jacob Bickhart.   Kuhnrod Viberg.
John Derer.

Charter was issued May 24, 1859.

15

CHARTER OFFICERS.

Edwin L. Knight, W. M.
Jacob Bickhart, S. W.
C. H. Viberg, J. W. This is the same who is named above as Kuhnrod.

OLIVE BRANCH LODGE, No. 248,

AT POE.

Dispensation dated January 25, 1859.

OFFICERS UNDER DISPENSATION.

Noah M. Grandstaff, W. M.
Judge Vaughn, S. W.
William Long, J. W.

CHARTER MEMBERS.

Joel Vaughn.	James Clark.
Judge Vaughn	Henry Ely.
Elias G. Coverdale.	Noah M. Grandstaff.
Lemuel N. Coverdale.	James Clark.
Ezra Maloney.	Warren L. Mills.
William F. Wood.	Jesse Heaton.
William Long.	

Charter was issued May 25, 1859.

CHARTER OFFICERS.

Noah M. Grandstaff, W. M.
Judge Vaughn, S. W.
William Long, J. W.

MONROEVILLE LODGE, No. 293,

AT MONROEVILLE.

Dispensation dated January 31, 1863.

OFFICERS UNDER DISPENSATION.

Jabez Shaffer, W. M.
John Shaffer, S. W.
James Weiler, J. W.

CHARTER MEMBERS.

Jabez Shaffer.   J. L. Younker.
James Weiler.   J. R. Robinson.
W. B. Rabbit.   John Shaffer.
A. Engle.   John Wilson.

Charter issued May 27, 1863.

CHARTER OFFICERS.

Jabez Shaffer, W. M.
John Shaffer, S. W.
James Weiler, J. W.

HARLAN LODGE, No. 206,

AT HARLAN OR MAYSVILLE.

Dispensation issued May 27, 1863.

OFFICERS UNDER DISPENSATION.

Peter S. Crisenberg, W. M.
Ira S. Skinner, S. W.
Marion C. Monger, J. W.

CHARTER MEMBERS.

Peter S. Crisenberg.   David Pattee.
Ira S. Skinner.   Jopata S. Sellers.
Marion C. Monger.   George Platter.
William Herrick   John Townsend.

Charter was issued May 25, 1864.

CHARTER OFFICERS

Peter S. Crisenberg, W. M.
Ira S. Skinner, S. W.
John Townsend, J. W.

NEWMAN LODGE, No. 376,

AT NEW HAVEN.

Dispensation dated January 27, 1868.

OFFICERS UNDER DISPENSATION

James Savage, W. M.
Allan H. Dougall, S. W.
Lycurgus S. Null, J. W.

CHARTER MEMBERS.

James Savage   Edwin Shirley.
Allan H. Dougall.   A. I. Williamson.
Lycurgus S. Null.   S. Houk.
J. E. Taylor.   George W. Linden.
J. E. McKendry.

Charter issued May 27, 1868.

CHARTER OFFICERS.

James Savage, W. M.
Allan H. Dougall, S. W.
Lycurgus S. Null, J. W.

Charter revoked by the Grand Lodge May 25, 1897.

HENRY KING LODGE, No. 382,

AT HUNTERTOWN.

Dispensation dated March 24, 1868.

18

OFFICERS UNDER DISPENSATION.

Theron M. Andrews, W. M.
Stephen A. Thornton, S. W.
James O. Beardsley, J. W.

CHARTER MEMBERS.

Peter Shoaff.
F. C. Bacon.
Corwin Phelps.
Ira. A. West.
Stephen A. Thornto..
James P. Bass.
Henry King.

Theron M. Andrews.
James O. Beardsley.
George W. Hand.
John Anderson.
James Fleming.
David McQuiston, Jr.

Charter issued May 25, 1869.

CHARTER OFFICERS.

Theron M. Andrews, W. M.
Stephen A. Thornton, S. W.
James O. Beardsley, J. W.

Charter surrendered December 3, 1881, on account of lack of interest and financial embarrassment.

FORT WAYNE CHAPTER, No. 19,

ROYAL ARCH MASONS.

A dispensation for organization was granted May 15, 1857, by the Grand Chapter of Indiana.

The officers U. D. were:
Henry Rudisil, Most Ex. High Priest.
James W. Borden, Excellent King.
Robert Brackenridge, Excellent Scribe.
Sol. D. Bayless, Secretary.

The charter was dated May 24th of the same year with the following as charter members. Sol. D. Bayless, Henry

Rudisil, Joseph Johnson, C. W. Aylesworth, Jas. Armiston, Jas. B. Shoaff, William Stevens, Henry Work, A. H. Weils, Fred Hamilton, Henry Wehmer, Charles Case, Sam'l H. Shoaff, I. Ayers and E. C. Nelson.

The elected officers were the same as those U. D., with the exception of Secretary, C. W. Aylesworth being chosen to that office.

Its first meetings were in Kiser's hall, moved to MacDougal block in 1868, and held its first meeting in the Temple February 24, 1886.

FORT WAYNE COMMANDERY, No. 4,
KNIGHTS TEMPLAR.

Dispensation was granted May 13, 1853, and charter September 19th, same year. The officers U. D. and elected under charter were the same.

Sol. D. Bayless, Eminent Commander.

James Collins, Generalissimo.

James High, Captain General.

S. I. Baldwin, Recorder.

The charter members were Sol. D. Bayless, John W. Smith, Francis S. Aveline, Benj. Saunders, Wm. Stewart, Christian Orff, J. N. Dubarry, John Hamilton, M. H. Taylor, Oscar N. Hinkle, James Collins, Saml. McElfatrick, S. John W. Underhill, John Spencer, Jas. M. Bratton, W. H. Loomis, H. S. Goodwin, D. J. Silver, Wm. Wert, Jos. A. Stelwagon, J. M. Boon, W. H. Newman.

Met first at Kiser's hall, then in Stewart's, and moved to MacDougal block in 1868, and its first meeting in the Temple was March 4, 1886.

Its dispensation antedated the Grand Council of Indiana, being from the Grand Master of the Templars of the United States, and its charter from the Grand Encampment U. S. at the Lexington Conclave, and it was one of the four commanderies that organized the Indiana Grand Commandery.

FORT WAYNE COUNCIL, No 4,

ROYAL AND SELECT MASTERS.

Dispensation was granted in Dec. 1855. The officers U. D. were Wm. Hacker, Illustrious Master; G. M. Porter, Deputy Ill. Master; Jas. Collins, Principal Conductor; Sol. D. Bayless Recorder.

The charter was dated May 20, 1856, with Jas. Collins, Sol. D. Bayless, Henry Rudisil, J. B. Shoaff, James W. Borden, G. M. Porter, J. W. Sullivan, Wm. Hacker, Ira C. Bond, C. P. Anderson, J. E. Houser, C. F. Fish, H. C. Lawrence and G. M. Freyberger as charter members.

The first elected officers were:

Sol. D. Bayless, Ill. Master.

Henry Rudisil, Dep. Ill. Master.

D. W. Maples, Prin. Conductor.

Samuel McElfatrick, Recorder.

First meetings were held at Kiser's hall, moved to Mac-Dougall's in 1868, and to the Temple in 1886.

It was the first Council instituted after the organization of the Grand Council of Indiana.

THE SCOTTISH RITE

LODGE OF PERFECTION.

A body was formed here some time prior to ours, having its authority from a non-recognized jurisdiction, known as the Cerneau branch of Masonry.

To counteract this movement and to stop its spread, a meeting was held in the Masonic Temple December 22, 1886, which resolved to make application, and requested a dispensation which was granted under date of March 12, 1887, for a Lodge of Perfection, 14 degrees. The first convocation U. D. was held October 26, 1887, and the ineffable grades, 4 to 14 were conferred on 43 candidates.

The charter was granted September 19, 1888, with William Geake, Thrice Potent G. M.; Chauncey B. Oakley,

Dep. G. M.; Alfred D. Cressler, S. G. W., and Quincy B. Hossler, J. G. W., and the lodge was constituted October 20, 1888, by Ill. Samuel B. Sweet, representative of the Ill. Gr. M. of Indiana.

The charter members were: Wm. W. Rockhill, N. S. Lenheim, Samuel B. Sweet, Christian B. Stemen, James Rogers, Joseph W. Bell, Joseph L. Gruber, James S. Gregg, John F. Wing, Ferd F. Boltz, Jos. C. Williard, Chas. A. Munson, Wm. Geake, Quincy A. Hossler, Ranald T. McDonald, Chauncey B. Oakley, George W. Pixley, Allen Zollars, Alfred D. Cressler, John Lillie, Jr., Jas. R. Bobo, Robert B. Allison, Elmore Y. Sturgis, Jacob J. Todd, Louis C. Davenport, Robert C. Bell.

It had a membership June 30th, 1897, of 484.

On the 4th of April, 1889, a meeting was held in the hall of the Lodge of Perfection for the purpose of arranging for a Council of Princes of Jerusalem, 15 to 16 degrees. The dispensation prayed for was granted to Darius Council April 9, 1889, and charter issued September 17, 1890. It was accepted May 14th, and the historical degrees, 15 to 16 conferred upon a class of 44, November 27, 1889.

The first officers were:

Henry W. Mordhurst, M. E. Sov. P. G. M.

John D. Olds, Deputy Master.

Thomas R. Marshall, Sen. G. Warden.

Henry C. Hanna, Jun. G. Warden.

The charter members were: Henry W. Mordhurst, Levi Griffith, Wm. W. Rockhill, George Gedfrey, Jos. W. Bell, John D. Olds, Samuel B. Sweet, Charles E. Orff, Jacob J. Todd, Marshall S. Mahurin, Thos. R. Marshall, Wm. Geake, Christian B. Stemen, Louis C. Davenport, George W. Moore, Jas. B. Williams, Thomas Meyer, Frank T. Waring, John Humphreys, Henry C. Hanna, Chas. E. Read, Hugh M. Diehl, E. Y. Sturgis, George W. Loag, George W. Pixley, John Lillie, Jr., DeMott C. Gardner, Wm. M. Glenn, Alfred Hattersley, John S. Stevens, Wm. P. Morris,

Marion Teagarden, Allen Zollars, John W. Hayden, Charles
A. Munson, Chas. A. Wilding, Jos. L. Gruber, Franklin T.
Wing, John H. Bass, Ferdinand F. Boltz, Joshua J. Williams,
Wilber F. Heath, Jas. P. Gray.

The membership June 30th, 1897, was 358.

A meeting was held March 22, 1897, to consider the
establishment of a Chapter of the Rose Croix. Thomas R.
Marshall was elected Most Wise and Perfect Master; Robert
S. Robertson, Venerable and Perfect Knight S. W., and
George L. Greenwalt, Ven. and P. K. J. W., and an application forwarded to the Supreme Council, but the dispensation has not yet been granted.

THE ORDER OF THE EASTERN STAR.

Nor must we neglect to mention our Sisters, the Daughters of Eve who have allied themselves with us.

Summit City Chapter No. 45, O. E. S., was organized
in 1882 by Grand Patron Willis D. Engle in Home Lodge hall.

The first officers were:

Mrs. M. Jennie Graham, Worthy Matron.
Levi Griffith, Worthy Patron.
Mrs. Sarah A. Griffith, Associate Matron.
Martin Connett, Treasurer.
Daniel W. Souder, Secretary.
The "Star Offices" were filled by:
Mrs. Nellie Umstead, Conductress.
Mrs. Maria Brooks as Esther.
Mrs. John Spitler as
Mrs. Eliza Connett.
Mrs. Emma Fleming.
Mrs. Joseph Bennett.

This chapter flourished and had a membership of about
75, and had its meetings in Home Lodge hall. Unfortunate
dissensions caused the surrender of its charter in the latter
part of 1885.

Shiloh Chapter, O. E. S. was instituted U. D. July 7, 1893, in the Temple, and under charter May 31, 1894, by Wm. H. Smythe Acting Grand Patron. The officers U. D. and also elected for the first year under the charter were:

Dr. Christian B. Stemen, Worthy Patron.
Laura B. Henry, Worthy Matron.
Louise Cotter, Associate Matron.
Wm. J. Probasco, Secretary.
Lydia Smith, Treasurer.
The "Star Officers" were:
Minnie E. Probasco, Conductress.
Alice M. Teagarden, Associate Conductress.
Norian McNutt, Adah.
Jennie Craig, Ruth.
Martha E. Wohlfort, Esther.
Harriet Stemen, Martha.
Louise McNutt, Electa.
Emeline McNutt, Warder.
Marion Teagarden, Sentinel.

The charter members were: Messrs. and Masdames J. M. Henry, C. B. Stemen, B. E. Cotter, W. J. Probasco, M. Teagarden, L. D. McNutt, W. C. McNutt, W. P. Smith, J. C. Craig, J. W. Clark, A. J. Kesler, J. M. Griffith, Herman Tapp, Mrs. Nellie Umstead, Mrs. Sarah D. Ziegler, Misses Norian McNutt, Martha E. Wohlfort and Harriet Stemen.

The chapter is flourishing with 110 members.

We make only brief mention of a so-called St. Mary's Lodge No. 14, F. and A. M., and a St. Paul's Chapter No. 8, R. A. M. in imitation of Ancient and Accepted Masonry, in charge of and conducted by those of the African race. Will the teachings of Masonry cause us to reach out our hands to them and call them "brethren?" Stranger happenings might occur.

The Valley of Fort Wayne, in addition to several offices in the Grand bodies of the United States, has furnished the following presiding officers for the Grand bodies of Indiana.

Sol. D. Bayless in Grand Lodge, Grand Chapter, Grand Council and Grand Commandery.

David P. Whedon, Andrew H. Hamilton and Samuel B. Sweet in Grand Commandery.

Henry W. Mordhurst in Grand Council and Grand Chapter R. A. M., and Edward O'Rourke in Grand Lodge.

The association for building the Masonic Temple was organized February 13, 1878, and a contract let for a magnificent building June 5th, 1879.

But after erecting one story it was found that the pattern was too large for the cloth—the contractors were swamped and gave up the contract after receiving estimates amounting to $34.597.75. Various efforts were made to go on with the building, one of them being a great lottery scheme, something on the plan of a church fair. A very large amount of perfume, known as "Satisfaction Boquet" was received in prizes, but the whole affair failed to smell altogether sweet.

The plans were changed, and by this change $37,000 was required to make the opera house ready for use, and $10,000 more for the upper stories for the use of the Masonic bodies.

The building and lot were bonded, and after a long delay, the Opera house was dedicated November 5, 1884, by a series of four Grand Operas given by the Emma Abbott Opera troupe, at the rate of ten dollars for a season ticket. The lodge rooms were not ready for occupancy till the beginning of 1886.

Thus I have tried to tell, as briefly as I could in Justice to the theme, the history of our Summit Valley. Much of it has been told before, much remains that could be told, but we believe it to be a record in which you all feel an interest and not a little of pride.

Many have gone before us into the Valleys beyond. All

of us are moving rapidly from the east to the west. Our eyes are turning from the rising to the setting sun.

We of the plains are accustomed to say of those gone before, "He has passed over the river." The dwellers among the mountains say, "He has gone over the divide," or, "beyond the range."

When we are called from this, our present vale, to pass over the river and climb the divide, may we find on the other side, valleys more beautiful, summits more grand, the valleys bright, fragrant, green and flowery, the mountain tops sheathed in silver, with the glory of gold and gems in the clouds that curtain them; and there, either upon the mountain top or in the secluded vale, a temple built upon the foundation of Fraternity, Charity and Love ineffable, where we shall receive the welcome of brethren, and the voice of the Grand Architect shall call us from labor to refreshment, from Earth's labor to Heaven's rest.

ROSTER

OF THE

.Masonic Lodges..

OF

ALLEN COUNTY, INDIANA.

ALSO

ort Wayne Chapter No. 19, Royal Arch Masons

ort Wayne Council No. 4, Royal   Select Masters

ort Wayne Commandery No. 4, Knights Templar

AND

ANCIENT AND ACCEPTED
SCOTTISH RITE MASONRY

Fort Wayne Lodge of Perfection

Darius Council, Princes of Jerusalem.

YORK RITE.

SYMBOLIC MASONRY.

Color. BLUE. Denotes friendship, and is the peculiar characteristic a Master Mason.

Calendar.—ANCIENT CRAFT MASONS commence their era with the creation of the world, calling it *Anno-Lucis* [A. L.], meaning " in the year of light." A. D. 1898 is 5898.

WAYNE LODGE No. 25, F. AND A. M

FORT WAYNE.

Instituted November 17th, 1823.

Stated Meetings Saturday on or before the full moon and every Saturday for work.

PAST WORSHIPFUL MASTERS

WITH YEARS OF SERVICE.

a. ALEXANDER EWING .... 1823.
b. GENERAL JOHN TIPTON .... 1823-24 25 26 27.
    JOSEPH HOLMAN .... 1828.
    LEWIS G. THOMPSON .... 1828.
    ANTHONY L. DAVIS .... 1829.
    HUGH HANNA .... 1830.
    ABSOLOM HOLCOMB .... 1830.
    SAMUEL HANNA .... 1831-32.
    HENRY RUDISILL .... 1833.
c. SAMUEL EDSALL .... 1833.

a. Appointed First Master.
b.- Elected First Master.
c. - Lodge work, irregularly from 1833 to 1857.
See Robertson's history, in this book, of Wayne Lodge.

— —

LIST OF MEMBERS.

Adams, William E.
Alden, Sam'l R.
Allen, George H.
Altevoght, Harry F.
Anderson, Oliver.
Armack, J. Bernard.
Armstrong, James A.
Ash, Henry J.
Ashley, George L.

Barrett, James M.
Barthold, Frederick L.
Barthold, Harry.
Baker, Josiah C. M.
Bash, Daniel F.
Belot, George E.
Bisel, Elmer E.
Bitner, John R.
Blade, Phillip.
Blitz, Max J.
Bond, Chas. E.

Borhek, Herman S.
Bowen, George R.
Brokaw, James H.

Cartwright, Porter.
Cavanagh, William.
Clark, Jacob W.
Cohen, Henry.
Cook, Ernest W.
Craig, James C.
Craig, James T.
Cratsley, Frank C.
Crawford, D. Frank.

Davidson, Charles S.
Dougall, John T.
Doughman, Newton D.
Downing, Myron.
Dunfee, Emmett W.
Durfee, George A.
Duryee, George W.

29

Eckert, David S.
Esry, Elwood T.
Ewing, George W.

Falls, Daniel M.
Fee, Frank F.
Fitch, Chas. B.
Foster, Andrew.

Gage, Robert.
Gould, Carrol C.
Gould, Theo. H.
Graham, James A.
Gray, James P.

Haberkorn, Henry.
Hall, Charles W.
Hall, Thomas N.
Hanna, Joseph T.
Harding, Daniel L.
Hanhardt, C. F.
Haslem, Alfred E.
Hebert, Oliver.
Heaton, Owen H.
Heller, George W.
Hill, Charles A.
Hile, Frederick.
Hollister, Edwin J.
House, James A.
Humphrey, James.

Johnston, David D.
Jump, Edward D.

Kanaga, Lee A.
Kelley, John B.
Keplinger, Frank E. D.
Kerr, William W.
Kimball, William R.
King, Frank E.
King, Josiah.
Kretsinger, Constantine.
Kretsinger, Henry R.
Kretsinger, John R.
Kuhne, Chas. W.

Law, Chas. D.
Law, Herbert J.
Lewis, James D.
Lipsett, William E.
Loomis, Ray M.
Lucas, Charles O.

Lumbard, Sidney C.
Lysinger, George P.

McCormick, Thomas H.
McDole, Henry G.
McMahon, Sylvester.
Miller, Isaac.
Miller, James E.
Minsky, Samuel.
Monia, Charles H.
Morris, John Jr.

Neal, Charles F.

O'Rourke, Edward.

Palmer, Earl.
Parker, Oliver P.
Phillips, George A.
Pierce, Everett.
Pierce, Harry W.
Pletz, J. Ferd.
Porter, Hiram.
Porter, Miles F.
Potter, George L.
Pottlitzer, Isadore.
Probasco, William J.

Ragan, Charles.
Randall, Perry A.
Reidelsheimer, David S.
Reinking, Frederick W.
Reitnour, Jacob.
Reul, John V.
Rider, Frank A.
Roberts, George.
Rodabaugh, John F.
Rodabaugh, Thomas J.
Rogers, Lamort M.
Romlike, Herman E.
Romy, Robert L.
Rosenthal, Morris.
Ross, George A.
Ross, John E.

Sauerbier, William A.
Sauers, James T.
Schied, Peter .
Sechler, Milo H.
Silverstein, Max.
Sine, Amos.
Siver, Emett L.

Sleat, Barry W.
Smith, Reader P.
Stahl, Charles F.
Stephan, Wilhelm.
Stotz, Ulrich.
Sutter, J. R.
Sutton, David.

Tapp, Ferdinand.
Taylor, George B.
Telley, George W.
Thieme, John A.
Thompson, Nelson.
Todd, Warner W.
Trythal, James.
Turner, John E.

Van Buskirk, Aaron F.
Vesey, William J.

Wallace, John.
Watt, William A.
Weil, Isaac.
Welsheimer, William T.
Wilding, Charles A.
Wilson, George H.
Wilson, George W.
Wilt, Frank P.
Witzigreuter, Max.
Wood, William C. Jr.
Woolever, Orla A.
Worch, Louis A.

SUMMIT CITY LODGE No. 170, F. AND A. M.

FORT WAYNE.

— —

Instituted June 9th, 1854.

Stated Meetings First Friday each month and every Friday for work.

PAST WORSHIPFUL MASTERS.

CHARLES CASE.........................June, 1854, to June, 1858.
FRANK S. AVELINE ....June, 1858, to June, 1859.
EDWARD L. FORCE....................June, 1859, t） June, 18 0.
WILLIAM H. NEWMAN................June, 1860, to June, 1861.
MUNSON VAN GIESON ....June, 1861, to June, 1862.
MORTIMER H. TAYLOR.................June, 1862, to November, 1862.
WILLIAM H. NEWMAN ....June, 1863, to June, 1866.
GEORGE W. VOORHIS.................June, 1866, to June, 1867.
WILLIAM H. NEWMAN ....June, 1867, to June, 1868.
M. B. STRONG.........................June, 1868, to December, 1869.
W. C. BABCOCK.......................December, 1869, to December, 1873.
SAMUEL B. SWEET.....,..............December, 1873, to December, 1874.
WILLIAM KNIGHT.....................December, 1874, to December, 1875.
C. L. THOMAS........................December 1875, to December 1876.
LEVI GRIFFITH.......................December, 1876, to December, 1880.
ROBERT A. LIGGET...................December, 1880, to December, 1881.
WILLIAM S. PATTEN..................December, 1881, to December, 1883.
SAMUEL B. SWEET ....December, 1883, to December, 1884.
JOHN T. LEACH.......................December, 1884, to December, 1886.
WILLIAM KNIGHT....................December, 1886, to December, 1887.
WILLIAM S. PATTEN..................December, 1887, to December, 1888.
WILLIAM GEAKE......................December, 1888, to December, 1890.
AMMON S. BRINTZENHOFF,...........December, 1890, to December, 1892.
EDGAR S. YOUNG ....December, 1892, to December, 1895.
WILLARD C. McNUTT ....December, 1895, to December, 1897.
JOHN W. McCAUSLAND ....December, 1897, to December, 1898.

LIST OF MEMBERS.

Adams, Charles C.
Allen, Alfred.
Allen, Cyrus.
Anderson, Andrew.
Andrews, James C.

Baer, Alvin E.
Baird, Clarence.
Baldwin, Merchant H.
Barber, Henry E.
Barden, William N.
Barnes, Charles A.
Barnett, Abraham G.
Barnett, Byron H.
Barnett, James W.
Bart, Nelson.
Bass, John H.
Beard, Milo.
Beard, Charles F.
Bell, George E.
Berget, Cyrus J.
Blair, Solon K.
Bloombaugh, Otto.
Bochlin, Frederick.
Bond, Charles Z.
Bourie, George W.
Bowers, George B. M.
Bowser, August.
Bradley, Edgar O.
Branstrattor, William.
Brill, Henry F.
Britzenhofe, Ammon S.
Brooks, Milo H.
Brown, John S.
Brumfield, William E.
Buchanan, Lawrence A.
Burrowes, Stephen A.

Cairns, James.
Carter, Isaac.
Cherry, William H.
Christiansen, Christian.
Clem, Isiah.
Coleman, Thomas.
Connelly, James T.
Couser, Charles.
Cowen, Millard.
Cressler, Alfred D.
Crow, John.

Cunnison, James.
Current, William A.

Dailey, Eph.
Dailey, Louis G.
Dalman, John.
Darker, George U.
Dawson, Charles M.
Dickson, James M.
Doty, Richard.
Doud, Wallace E.
Drake, Thomas.

Eckart, Charles.
Edwards, Daniel.
Eicks, Louis.
Eldred, Danford P.
Empie, Thomas B.

Felts, George K.
Fischer, Henry E.
Fisher, George H.
Fisk, William.
Flack, Charles R.
Fleming, Thomas H.
Foulke, Albert G.
Fox, Frank.

Galliher, James G.
Garman, John W.
Geake, William.
Geake, William C.
Germain, Ross M.
Gilbert, Charles W.
Gillette, C. M.
Gillie, James.
Ginty, Michael O.
Glenn, William M.
Goodman, William.
Goslee, Samuel.
Greer, Thomas Jr.
Greer, Thomas Sr.
Griffith, James M.
Griffith, Levi.
Grout, William.

Hamlet, Jesse.
Hanna, Henry C.
Harrod, Morse.
Harper, James B.

33

Harper, Lorenzo V.
Harsh, George.
Hazzard, Albert.
Henehen, Edward.
Henderson, A. H.
Henry, James M.
Hewes, James C.
Hockaday, Warren.
Hoffman, A. Ely.
Hoffman, G. Max.
Holland, Robert.
Houder, Martin L.
Hudgel, Resin D.
Hue, Constantine L.
Hulcher, Frank.

Johnson, James T.
Jones Edward S.

Kemp, Edgar.
Kemp, Herbert.
Kendrick, Charles.
Kenerk, Edward.
Keppel, Charles H.
Kerlin, William L.
Ketler, Conrad F.
Kilpatrick, James.
Kimmel, John.
Kirchifer, Herman A.
Kitselman, William B.
Knight, Thomas C.
Knight, William.
Kyle, Abraham.

Lackey, Melvin.
Leach, John T.
Leonard, James H.
Ligget, Robert A.
Liscum, John R.
Long, James B.
Lorton, Jesse G.

McCausland, John W.
McDarman, James E.
McFerran, John A.
McKay, David.
McKean, John.
McMillan, James.
McNaught, Duncan.
McNutt, Henry F.
McNutt, Willard.
McQuiston, Wilson.

Madison, William J.
Manchester, Alfred E.
Markey, Adolph J.
Match, John.
Metcalf, Samuel S.
Metzner, Jasper.
Miller, John M.
Moore, George W.
Moore, Samuel C.
Morris, William P.
Morris, William S.
Moses, Frank D.
Mossman, Paul B.
Mossman, William E.
Mottinger, Samuel.
Munson, Charles A.

Neidhart, Henry.
Newton, Charles H.

Orff, Charles E.
Orr, John W.
Orrock, William W.

Patton, William S.
Poihamus, Albert H.

Rabus, Gustave A.
Ravhouser, Richard C. F.
Read, Charles E.
Rehorst, Frederick.
Reiter, George.
Reynolds, Homer B.
Riblet, Hiram F.
Richardson, James A.
Roberts, Andrew V.
Rogers, Henry O.
Rogers, James.
Root, Vandorn.
Ross, Richard M.
Rossington, Rodolphus B.
Rossington, William.

Sauer, Carl.
Sautter, Frederick W.
Schiefer, Christian.
Schlatter, Noah.
Schrader, W. Frank.
Scott, Arza.
Scott, George.
Scott, George M.
Scott, George T.

Scott, James.
Scott, John.
Seaton, Robert L.
Shaffer, Frank H.
Shaffer, George.
Shaffer, Isaac.
Smith, Andrew J.
Smith, Willard P.
Szink, George A.
Sweringen, Bud Van.
Sweringen, Frank H
Sweet, Darwin.
Sweet, Samuel B.
Sweet, Frank.
Swartz, John Ard.
Stouder, Frank E.
Stouder, Henry G.
Stouder, Jacob M.
Stevens, Joseph J.
Sponhauer, Weidler S.
Spencer, George W.
Spencer, William H.
Souder, Daniel.
Sopher, Herbert.
Sleeper, Frank P.
Slater, John.
Shryock, William W.
Shoaff, Uriah S.
Shilling, Carl.
Shell, Jacob H.
Shaw, Albert P.

Talmage, Charles H.
Teagarden, Claude A.
Teagarden, Harvey.
Teagarden, Marion.
Thomas, Eugene.

Thompson, George.
Thompson, John W.
Thompson, Laughlin W.
Thompson, Richard G.
Timmis, William.
Titus, Charles.
Todd, John S.
Tresselt, Charles.

Umstead, Hiram D.
Urbahns, C. Emil.

Van Gorder, Charles.
Van Slyke, Ira M.
Vollmer, William C.

Wallace, Andrew.
Waltemath, William L.
Waterman, Andrew O.
Ward, William.
Weatherhogg, Charles R.
Webster, Benjamin H.
Welch, Daniel L.
Wheeler, Robert B.
White, Alexander B.
Wilkens, Christian.
Wilkens, Jacob V.
Wilson, Frank W.
Wright, James M.

You, Adolph J.
Young, Edward S.

Zeigler, Charles W.
Zumbro, Harry W.
Zumbro, William L.

1126005

35

LEO LODGE No. 224, F. AND A. M.

LEO.

Instituted January 10th, 1859.

Stated Meetings Wednesday on or before the full moon and every Wednesday for work.

PAST MASTERS

WITH YEARS OF SERVICE.

EDWARD L. KNIGHT .... 1859 until 1868 inclusive.
ELIAS ZIMMERMAN .... 1869 70-71 73 75.
EDGAR KEMP .... 1872 74.
JOHN W. HOLLOPETER .... 1876 77 78 81 82 83.
CHARLES GODFREY .... 1879 80.
CHRISTIAN J. SCHLATTER .... 1884 85 86 89-90-97.
MATHIAS HOLLOPETER .... 1887-88 96.
EUGENE COOK .... 1891 92.
WILLIAM C. HOLLOPETER .... 1893 94-98.
WILLIAM M. DEPEW .... 1895.

LIST OF MEMBERS.

Amstutz, John Sr.

Carlton, John.
Chapman, Solomon C.
Cook, Reuben.

Depew, William M.

Eby, Marks.
Eckles, John H.
Emanuel, Markus C.

Hollopeter, Mathias.
Hollopeter, William C.

Myers, Nelson.

Schlatter, Christian.
Schlatter, David D.

Viberg, George H.

36

OLIVE BRANCH LODGE No. 248, F. AND A. M.

POE.

Instituted January 25th, 1859.

Stated Meetings Thursday on or before the full moon, and every Tuesday for work.

PAST MASTERS.

WITH YEARS OF SERVICE.

NOAH M. GRANDSTAFF..... .1859 60 61 62.
JOEL VAUHN................1863 64 65.
EZRA MALANY..............1866 67.
JESSE HEATON.............1868 69-70 71 72 73 74 75 78 79 80 82 83 84-88.
MORGAN HARROD,...........1876 77.
ANDREW J. EMERICK........1881.
JAMES B. EMERICK.........1885 89 90 91 92 93.
HARVEY K. TURNER.........1886 87.
THOMAS MULLEN ....1894 95.
JACOB L. EMERICK.........1896-97-98.

LIST OF MEMBERS.

Archibald, John M.

Carles, Horace W.
Cartwright, Andrew.
Cartwright, Joseph.
Cartwright, Rollin.
Chapman, Frank M.
Chapman, Preston.
Comer, William.

Deel, George.

Ellenwood, Horace D.
Emerick, Elza O.

Emerick, Emmett V.
Emerick, George W.
Emerick, Jacob.
Emerick, Jacob L.
Emerick, James B.
Emerick, Judson B.

Fisher, Jacob.

Garton, James B.
Gibson, Arthur M.

Hatch, Lewis.
Hiser, George.

King, Asa
King, John.
King, Thomas.
Kreigh, Abraham.

LaFollete, George W.
Lechner, J. Alvin.

Mullen, Thomas.

Nireiter, Andrew.

Scott, William.
Snider, Preston.

Snider, Solomon Jr.
Somers, Edward.
Somers, Levi.
Somers, William H.
Sprang, Miio J.

Thurber, Mark.
Trenary, John.
Turner, Harvey K.

Vanhorn, William.

MONROEVILLE LODGE No. 293, F. AND A. M.

MONROEVILLE.

Instituted January 31st, 1863.

Meets First and Third Wednesdays of each month.

PAST MASTERS.

WITH YEARS OF SERVICE.

JABEZ SHAFFER............1863-64.
MARTIN E. ARGO...   1865-66-67 68.
ALPHEUS SWIFT.... .   1869-70-71.
GEORGE WEBSTER........1872.
JACOB SWANEY........ ....1873-74.
WILLIAM DICKERSON......1875.
WILLIAM T. WILSON.......1876.
AMASSA S. ROBINSON.....1877-78-79-80-81-83-84-86 88-89-91-92-93-94-95-96-97-98
JACOB CASSIDY.....   1882.
HENRY SMITH......   .1885 87-90.

LIST OF MEMBERS.

Alliger, John D.

Baker, George.
Baker, William D.
Barto, Daniel.
Bates, Charles.
Bauserman, Isiah.

Dickerson, William.
Doggett, Alcibides.
Fredline, Emanuel.

Jones, Thomas S.

Magner, William.
Maxheimer, John H.
Maxheimer, William.
May, Daniel A.
Murchland, William.

Nash, John P.
Nill, Charles A.
Nill, Thomas A.

Purman, David C.
Purman, Samuel B.

Robison, Amasa S.

Shaffer, Amasa J.
Staunton, Mortimer F.
Strauss, Julius M.
Strauss, Morris.
Smith, Henry.

Webster, Frank S.
Webster, George.
Wellbaum, Joseph L.
Wilson, William T.

39

HARLAN LODGE No. 296, F. AND A. M.

HARLAN.

Instituted May 27th, 1863.

Stated Meetings on Friday before the full moon; every Friday for work.

PAST MASTERS.

WITH YEARS OF SERVICE.

PETER S. CRISENBERG................1863 to 1880.
JOHN STOPHER......................1881-82-83-84 85-86-87-88-89-90-93-95-97-98.
ROBERT R. MURPHY.................1891-92.
JAMES NUTTLE......................1896.
WILLIAM OBERHOLZER ....1894.

--- --

LIST OF MEMBERS.

Adams, Horace E.
Austin, Andrew W.

Darling, George W.

Farner, Noah.

Grubb, Ira J.

Heath, Stephen.
Hood, Frank M.
Hood, Thomas.

Jones, Samuel N.

Murphy, Robert R.

Nuttle, James.

Oberholzer, William.
Obyer, David N.

Richart, Joseph.

Shaffer, John.
Sharp, Lewis.
Sheppleman, Henry.
Small, John.
Stopher, John.

Thimbler, John,

Wells, Joseph C.
Wilber, George W.
Walker, Edwin.

SOL. D. BAYLESS LODGE No. 359,
F. AND A. M.

FORT WAYNE.

Instituted June 4th, 1866.

Stated Meetings Second Monday each month and every Monday for work.

PAST MASTERS.

WITH YEARS OF SERVICE.

BYRON D. ANGELL	1866.
JOHN M. COOMBS	1867.
ANSON WARING	1868.
WILLIAM JOHNSON, JR.	1869-70-71.
JOHN I. WHITE	1872-73-74.
GEORGE D. CRANE	1875.
WILLIAM JONNSON, JR	1876.
EDWARD L. CRAW	1877.
ANDREW R. McCURDY	1878.
JOHN I. WHITE	1879.
CHAUNCEY B. OAKLEY	1880.
BENJAMIN M. HERR	1881.
GEORGE K. TORRENCE	1882.
ANDREW R. McCURDY	1883.
CHAUNCEY B. OAKLEY	1884-85.
EDWARD L. CRAW	1886.
CHAUNCEY B. OAKLEY	1887.
CHRISTIAN B. STEMEN	1888.
ALBERT BANISTER	1889.
CHRISTIAN B. STEMEN	1890-91.
CHARLES D. TILLO	1892.
CHARLES L. CARTER	1893-94-95-96.
ROBERT J. HAMILTON	1897.
CHARLES L. CARTER	1898.

LIST OF MEMBERS.

Aiken, Henry W. I.
Allen, Richard.
Archer, Charles E.
Atterbury, William W.

Bash, Harry E.
Bash, Winfield S.
Bauer, John J.
Beck, James.
Bender, Jacob G.
Bird, Ochmig.
Bittinger, Adam H.
Blakesley, John H.
Brinsley, George E. Jr.
Brinsley, John C.
Brown, James D.
Buchman, Alpheus, P.

Carter, Charles L.
Cassady, George M.
Caswell, Frank A.
Coimey, Christian R.
Cook, Clarence F.
Coverdale, Arabel S.
Crane, George D.
Craw, Edward L.
Croxton, Worthington A.

Dartnell, William E.
Diether, Louis.
Donivan, John W.
Doyle, D. M.

Edmunds, Frank W.
Edsall, William E.
Enslen, William M.
Ensminger, Ott D.
Estry, Albert G.
Evans, George P.
Evans, John P.
Evans, Josiah.

Fahnestock, James W.
Fay, Montford W.
Flagle, Milton G.
Foote, W. Albert.
Foster, Nathaniel H.
Frank, Theodore.
Frankel, Louis.

Friend, Alfred I.
Friend, Henry.
Friend, Jacob.

Gates, Horatio S.
Gilbert, John.
Granger, Horace G.
Granneman, Henry C.
Green, Seth F.
Greenawalt, George I.
Greensfelder, Josiah.
Griffith, Chauncey L.

Hamilton, Robert J.
Hanna, J. Thomas.
Hanna, Oliver S.
Hanna, Robert B.
Harper, Benjamin F.
Hartman, George B.
Hartman, S. Brenton.
Hattersley, Alfred.
Havice, Samuel H.
Heit, Anthony W.
Hetrick, Jacob A.
Higgins, Cecilius R.
Hilgeman, Franklin H.
Hilgeman, Henry F.
Huguenard, Frank A.
Hood, William Ewing.
Horstman, R. Frank.
Hitchcock, H. W.

Jones, George A.
Jones, Harry A.
Jones, Maurice L.

Kelker, Anthony.
Kesler, Abraham J.
Learmonth, Robert.
Levy, Abraham.
Lichtenwalter, Albert L.
Lichtenwalter, Charles C.
Loesch, George H.
Loveless, Walter H.

McCurdy, Andrew R.
McDonald, Emmet H.
Meers, Robert A.
Miller, Clarence C.
Miller, Frederick M.

42

Minto, Archibald O. Jr.
Mitchell, Robert B.
Morgan, George W.
Moritz, Harry L.

Nathan, Charles.

Oakley, Chauncey B.
Ogle, John J.
Olds, Henry G.
Osborn, Merlin C.

Page, William D.
Paulus, Frank D.
Phipps, John A.
Plantinga, Peter.
Potter, Phillip L.
Pyke, Charles W.

Rabus, George J.
Redlich, Joseph.
Reid, Charles S.
Reese, Lyman B. B.
Rockhill, William W.
Rossell, Joseph A.
Rupprecht, H. W.
Rurode, Ernest C.

Seaman, J. W.
Shambaugh, William H.
Sites, Edward F.

Smith, Henry T.
Smith, Persifor F. Jr.
Snyder, John.
Stahl, William G.
Steger, Gustave C. E.
Stemen, Christian B.
Stemen, George C.
Sterling, Reynolds.
Stone, Lester E.
Sweet, Edward R.

Thompson, Frank.
Thompson, Peter A.
Tibbles, Frank E.
Tillo, Charles D.
Tolan, Brentwood L.
Trenam George E.

Updike, Jacob V.

Walton, Joseph R.
Ward, George.
Webb, Marion A.
Weisell, David D.
Wherry, William P.
White John I.
Williams, Joshua J.
Wood, Paul E.

Zollars, Allen.

HOME LODGE No. 342, F. AND A. M.

FORT WAYNE.

Instituted July 17th, 1868.

Stated Meetings First Tuesday in each month, and every Tuesday for work.

PAST MASTERS

WITH YEARS OF SERVICE.

ORIN D. HURD	1868-69-70-71.
DANIEL GIBSON	1872-73.
JOSEPH WHAN	1874-75.
MANFORD M. SMICK	1876-77-92.
CHRISTIAN BOSEKER	1878-79.
JAMES E. GRAHAM	1880-81-85.
FRANK GIBSON	1882-83.
HENRY W. MORDHURST	1884-93-94.
FERDINAND C. BOLTZ	1886-87.
ISAAC W. BAKER	1888-89.
LOUIS C. KASTEN	1890-91.
JOSEPH E. SUNDERLAND	1895-96-97-98.

LIST OF MEMBERS.

Arnold, Amos W.

Baker, Isaac W.
Bassett, William O.
Bassett, John M.
Beamer, W. Bruce.
Bennett, Homer A.
Boseker, Christian
Boylan, John
Brinsley, Charles M.
Brown, John B.
Buckles, William T.
Bursley, George E.

Cameron, Glen.
Chadwick, John M.
Chadwick, Joseph P.
Collier, Amon B.
Cooper, George J.
Creighton, William.
Culbertson, Frank V.

Davis, William A.
Deady, Emmett.
Deahl, Frederick T.
Detzer, Gustave G.
Develin, William C.

44

Dull, Daniel J.
Dunlop, Andrew W.

Eagy, John H.

Fally, William W.
Fields, William S.
Flack, Cyrus I.

Gable, Peter.
Gair, Joseph.
Gage, Henry C.
Gardner, DeMotte C.
Gary, William T.
Gavin, James.
Gibson, Frank.
Gillespie, R. R.
Godfrey, George L.
Gumprer, Jacob D.
Graham, James E.
Greene, Richard B.
Grindle, Alfred.
Griswold, Crawford.
Gruber, Joseph L.

Hattersley, Willis.
Hayden, John W.
Heit, Christopher.
Henline, Samuel.
Henstock, Arthur.
Hilt, Fred.
Hoham, Fred. D.
Hollsworth, A.
Hull, Sylvester W.
Hurd, Orrin D.

Jacobs, Miron N.
Johns, Alfred L.
Johnson, Thomas J.

Kasten, Louis C.
Kensill, George.
Kiefer, Adolph.
Kinerk, William.
Kikley, Paul I.
King, William L.
Kitzelman, John.
Kleint, August G.
Klippert, George.
Kreuper, August E.
Kuhne, H. Richard.

Lapp, Charles J.
Lancaster, Charles.
Lauferty, Alex S.
Liebman, Ernest F.
Link, Addison.
Lomas, Charles.
Lomas, Edward.

Malott, Calvin.
McCulloch, Charles.
McCracken, James K.
Miller, George T.
Morgan, John B.
Mordhurst, Henry W.
Mollett, Henry L.
Muirhead, Alexander.

Nathan, Julius.
Niswonger, Henry W.
Nirdlinger Joseph.

Olds, John D.

Poyser, Hiram.

Raugh, Gustave A.
Robertson, Robert S.
Robinson, James M.
Ross, Edward C.
Ross, Judson K.
Rowe, William.

Sawyer, Charles S.
Schoch, August F.
Seidel, Edward.
Shell, E. Clarence.
Shoof, Frederick S.
Smick, Manford M.
Smick, Stanton S.
Smith, Charles H.
Smead, Frank K.
Staub, Alexander.
Stilson, George W.
Stover, George W.
Strass, Isaac.
Strauss, Leo.
Sunderland, Joseph E.

Tresselt, Fred T.
Thompson, Benjamin F.

45

Walter, Amos R.
Walter, Harry H.
Walter, Eyer.
Ward Charles C.
Warner, Thomas C.
Weigel, Jacob W.
Weitzel, Walter W.
Whitmore, William T.

Wilson, William R.
Wilding, James A.
   (Died April 7, 1898.)
Wyatt, Henry M.

Yost, George T.

Vordermark, John W.

CAPITULAR MASONRY.

Color.--SCARLET Denoting Zeal—that fervency and zeal that should actuate all Regular Royal Arch Masons.

Calendar.— ROYAL ARCH MASONS date from the year the second Temple was commenced by Zerubbabel, or 530 B. C. *Anno-Inventionis* [A. Inv.], meaning the "Year of the Discovery." A. D. 1898 A. Inv. 2428.

FORT WAYNE CHAPTER No. 19, ROYAL ARCH MASONS.

Instituted May 24th, 1851.

Stated Meetings First Wednesday in each month, and every Wednesday for work.

PAST HIGH PRIESTS

WITH YEARS OF SERVICE.

HENRY RUDISIL	1851.
JAMES COLLINS	1852-53-54-55.
SOL D. BAYLESS	1856-59-65-67.
CHARLES CASE	1857.
JOSEPH JOHNSON	1858-61-63.
SAMUEL McELFATRICK	1860-62-64.
GEORGE VOORHIS	1866.
JOSEPH FREEMAN	1868.
WILLIAM T. FOSTER	1869-70.
ORSON SMITH	1871.
ANDREW H. HAMILTON	1872-73.
JOSEPH A. STELLWAGON	1874-75.
SAMUEL B. SWEET	1876.
DANIEL L. HARDING	1877.
MANFORD M. SMICK	1878-79.
CHARLES M. DAWSON	1880.

James E. Graham	1881.
Henry W. Mordhurst	1882-83.
Allan H. Dougall	1884-85.
William Geake	1886-87-88.
James M. Henry	1889-90.
Levi Griffith	1891-92.
Ernest P. Leibman	1893.
Joseph L. Gruber	1894.
Robert A. Ligget	1895.
Alepander M. Tower	1896.
Joseph E. Sunderland	1897.
Willard C. McNutt	1898.

LIST OF MEMBERS.

Adams, Charles C.
Alden, Samuel R.
Allison, Robert B.
Altevogt, Henry F.
,Argo, Martin E.
Ashley, George,
Astry, Jonas.

Baer, Alvin E.
Barnett, Abraham G.
Barnett, Byron H.
Barrett, James M.
Bass, John H.
Bauer, John J.
Beamer, Willliam Bruce.
Bedson, John H.
Belott, George E.
Birget, Cyrus J.
Blair, Solon K.
Blitz, Maximilian J.
Boltz, Ferdinand F.
Bond, Charles E.
Bond, Charles Z.
Boen, James M.
Boseker, Christian.
Brew, Nicholas.
Brinsley, Charles M.
Brinsley, John C.
Brintzenhofe, Amon S.
Brown J. Linville.
Buchman, Alpheus P.
Bulson, Albert E.

Cameron, Glenn.
Chadwick, John M.

Clark, Jacob W.
Collier, Amon B.
Cooper, George J.
Cotter, Bartlett E.
Craig, James C.
Crane, George D.
Cressler, Alfred D.
Current, William A.

Dawkins, Henry E.
Detzer, Gustave G.
Dickson, James M.
Donivan, John W.
Doty, Richard E.
Dougall, Allan H.
Douglass, Robert F.
Durfee, George A.

Eckart, David S.
Emrick, Emmet V.
Enslen, William.
Everett, Charles E.

Falley, William W.
Fee, Frank F.
Fields, William S.
Fitch, Charles B.
Flack, Charles R.
Flagle, Milton G.
Foote, William A.
Fox, Frank.

Gardner, DeMotte C.
Gavin, James A.
Geake, William.

48

Germain, Ross M.
Gillie, James.
Ginty, Michael O.
Glenn, William M.
Godfrey, Charles.
Godfrey, George L.
Gould, Theodore H.
Graham, James E.
Granger, Horace.
Gray, James P.
Greenawalt, George L.
Griffith, James M.
Griffith, Levi.
Grout, William H.
Gruber, Joseph L.

Hanna, Henry C.
Harding, Daniel L.
Hayden, John W.
Heaton, Owen N.
Hebert, Oliver.
Heit, Anthony W.
Henderson, Andrew R.
Henstock, Arthur S.
Henry, James M.
Hezlep, Alva C.
Higgins, Cecilius R.
Hilton, Charles S.
Hockady, Joseph W.
Hollister, Edwin J.
Houder, Martin L.
Howes, David.
Hudgel, Rezin D.
Hue, Constant L.
Hughes, James H.
Hurd, Orin D.

Jones, Maurice L.

Kassel, Louis.
Kasten, Louis C.
Keeler, Joseph W.
Kerlin Wm L.
Kesler, Abraham J.
Kiefer, Adolph.
Kimball, William R.
Kirkpatrick, Charles A. L.
Kleint, August G.
Knight, William.
Kretsinger, John R.
Krueper, August E.
Kyle, Abram P.

Larimore, Miles H.
Lauferty, Alexander S.
Law, Charles D.
Law, Herbert J.
Lewis, James D.
Lickley, Newton A.
Liebman, Ernest F.
Ligget, Robert A
Lipset, William E.
Liscum, John R.
Loesch, George H.
Lomas, Charles.
Lorton, Jesse G.

Manchester, Albert E.
Mauk, Frances M.
Metzner, Jasper.
Miller, John M.
Moore, George W.
Mordhurst, Henry W.
Morgan, Joseph D.
Morris, William P.
Moses Frank D.
Munson, Charles A.
McArdle, George.
McCausland, John W.
McCulloch, Charles.
McDonald, Ranald T.
McElfatrick, John B.
McKay, David.
McMahon, Sylvester.
McMillan, James.
McNutt, Willard C.

Nickey, Addison B.
Null, Lycurgus S.

Oakley, Chauncey B.
Olds, John D.
Orff, Charles F.
Orrock, William W.

Palmer, Earl.
Polhamus, Andrew H.
Pond, Alen J.
Probasco, William J.

Rabus, George.
Read, Charles E.
Reiter, George.
Riblett, Hiram F.
Richardson, James A.

49

Rider, Frank A.
Rockhill, William W.
Ross, Edward C.
Rossington, Rodolphus B.

Sauers, James T.
Schrader, William F.
Shambaugh, William H.
Simonson, James H.
Sine, Amos.
Sites, Frank E.
Slater John.
Sleeper, Frank P.
Smead, Frank K.
Smick, Manford M.
Smith, Reader.
Smith, Willard P.
Spencer, George W.
Staub, Alex H.
Stemen, George C.
Stouder, Frank E.
Stouder, Jacob M.
Straus, Leopold.
Sunderland, Joseph E.
Sweet, Samuel B.
Szink, George A.

Tapp, Herman W.
Teagarden, Marion.

Thompson, Frank.
Thompson, Nelson W.
Tillo, Charles D.
Titus, Charles H.
Tolan, Brentwood S.
Turner, Harvey K.

Umstead, Hiram D.

VanSlyke, Ira M.
Vesey, William J.

Wallace, John.
Welsheimer, William T.
Wheeler, Robert B.
White, John I.
Wilding, Charles A.
Wilding, James W.
   (Died April 7, 1898.)
Wilkens, Christian.
Wilkens, Jacob V.
Wilt, Frank P.
Wing, John F.
Wood Paul E.
Worch, Louis A.

Zollars, Allan.

CRYPTIC MASONRY.

Color.—PURPLE Denoting Unity, being a due admixture of blue and scarlet, and is to remind us to cultivate a spirit of fraternal union.

Calendar.—ROYAL AND SELECT MASTERS date from the year the Temple of Solomon was completed. *Anno-Depositionis* [A. Dep.], or " In the Year of the Deposit." A. D. 1898 A. Dep. 2898.

FORT WAYNE COUNCIL No. 4,
ROYAL AND SELECT MASTERS.

Instituted May 20th, 1856.

Stated Meetings Second Wednesday in each month, and every Wednesday for work.

PAST ILLUSTRIOUS MASTERS.

WITH YEARS OF SERVICE.

SOL D BAYLESS............................1856-57-58.
JOSEPH JOHNSON,.........................1859-60-61-62-63-64.
MUNSON VAN GIESON ....Unexpired Term 1864 and 69.
JOSEPH FREEMAN..........................1865-66-70.
GEORGE VOORHIS...........................1867.
BYRON D. ANGELL........................1868.
SAMUEL H. SHOAFF.......................1871.
JOSEPH A. STELLWAGON..................1872-73-76-77.
ANDREW H. HAMILTON....................1874.
ORSON SMITH..............................1875.
SAMUEL B. SWEET.........................1878.
MANFORD M. SMICK.......................1879-80.
HENRY W. MORDHURST....................1881-83-84-85.
ALLAN H. DOUGALL.......................1882-86.
CHRISTIAN B. STEMEN....................1887-88.
LEVI GRIFFITH............................1889-90-93.

51

LIST OF MEMBERS.

Allison, Robert B.
Altevogt, Henry F.
Astry, Jonas.

Barnett, Abraham G.
Barnett, Byron H.
Bauer, John J.
Bell, Charles W.
Beil, Thomas H.
Belott, George E.
Blitz, Maximilian J.
Boltz, Ferdinand F.
Brew, Nicholas.

Chadwick, John M.
Clark, Jacob W.
Cooper, George J.
Cotter, Bartlett E.
Craig, James C.
Cressler, Alfred D.
Current, William A.

Doty, Richard E.
Dougall, Allan H.

Emrick, Emmett V.
Enslen, William.
Everett, Charles E.

Flack, Charles R.
Flagle, Milton G.
Foote, William A.

Gardner, LeMotte C.
Germain, Ross M.
Gillie, James.
Glenn, William M.
Godfrey, George L.
Gould, Theodore H.
Gray, James P.
Greenawalt, George L.
Griffith, James M.

Griffith, Levi.
Grout, William H.
Gruber, Joseph L.

Hattersley, Alfred.
Hebert, Oliver.
Henry, James M.
Hezlep, Alva C.
Hockaday, Joseph W.
Howes, David.
Hudgel, Rezin D.
Hue, Constant L.
Hughes, James H.
Hurd, Orin D.

Jones, Maurice L.

Kiefer, Adolph.
Kimball, Wm. R.

Lauferty, Alexander S.
Law, Herbert J.
Lickley, Newton A.
Liebman, Ernest F.
Ligget, Robert A.
Loesch, George H.
Lorton, Jesse G.

Metzner, Jasper.
Moone, George.
Moore, George W.
Mordhurst, Henry W.
Morgan, Joseph D.
Morris, William P.
Moses, Frank D.
Munson, Charles A.
McCausland, John W.
McCracken, James K.
McDonald, Ranald T.
McKay, David.
McNutt, Willard C.

52

Oakley, Chauncey B.
Olds, John D.

Pixley, George W.
Probasco, William J.

Rabus, George.
Redelsheimer, David S.
Reiter, George.
Riblett, Hiram F.
Richardson, James A.
Ross, Edward C.

Simonson, James H.
Sine, Amos.
Smick, Manford M.
Smith, Reader.
Spencer, George W.
Stemen, Christian B.
Stemen, George C.

Stouder, Frank E.
Straus, Leopold.
Sunderland, Joseph E.
Sweet, Samuel B.
Szink, George A.

Tapp, Herman W.
Teagarden, Marion.

Umstead, Hiram D.

VanSlyke, Ira M.

Wheeler, Robert B.
Wilding, Charles A.
Wilkens, Christian.
Wing, John F.
Wood, Paul E.

Zook, D. C.

CHIVALRIC MASONRY.

Color—BLACK AND WHITE. Referring to the color of banner carried by the Ancient Knights Templar to battle; one-half being white and the other black, signifying they were fair and favorable to the friends of Christ, dark and terrible to his enemies.

Calendar— KNIGHTS TEMPLAR commence their era with the organization of the Order, 1118 A. D. *Anno-Ordinis* [A. O.], "In the Year of the Order." A. D. 1898 A. O. 780.

FORT WAYNE COMMANDERY No. 4, KNIGHTS TEMPLAR.

Instituted September 19th, 1853.

Stated Meetings Third Thursday in each month, and every Thursday for work.

PAST COMMANDERS.

WITH YEARS OF SERVICE.

SOL D. BAYLESS	1853-54-58-59-61.
JAMES COLLINS	1855-57.
HENRY RUDISIL	1859.
SAMUEL McELFATRICK	1860-61-62.
CHARLES CASE	1863.
GEORGE VOORHIS	1864.
DAVID P. WHELDON	1865.
BYRON D. ANGELL	1866.
SAMUEL H. SHOAFF	1867.
JOSEPH A. STELLWAGON	1868-69.
ANDREW H. HAMILTON	1870.
CHARLES S. BRACKENRIDGE	1871-80.
JOHN H. BASS	1872.
ORIN D. HURD	1873-74.

LIST OF MEMBERS.

Allison, Robert B.
Altevogt, Henry F.

Barnett, Abraham G.
Barrett, James M.
Bass, John H.
Beamer, William B.
Bedson, John H.
Bond, Charles Z.
Boon, James M.
Boseker, Christian.
Brinsley, Charles M.
Brinsley, John C.
Brown, Alfred J.
Buchman, Alpheus P.

Chadwick, John M.
Clark, Jacob W.
Collier, Amon B.
Commoncavish, Feiix.
Cooper, George J.
Cotter, Bartlett F.
Craig, James C.
Cressler, Alfred D.
Current, William A.

Dickson, James M.
Donivan, John W.
Durfee, George A.

Emrick, Emmet V.
Everett, Charles E.

Fields, William E.
Fitch, Charles B.
Foote, William A.

Gardner, DeMotte C.
Gavin, James A.
Geake, William.
Germain, Ross M.
Gillie, James.
Ginty, Michael O.
Glenn, Thomas M.
Glenn, William M.
Godfrey, Charles.
Godfrey, George L.
Gould, Theodore H.
Granger, Horace G.
Gray, James P.
Griffith, James M.
Griffith, Levi.
Grout, William H.
Gruber, Joseph L.

Hanna, Henry C.
Hattersley, Alfred.
Hattersley, Willis.
Hayden, John W.

55

Hebert, Oliver.
Henderson, Andrew R.
(Died May 15, 1898.)
Henry, James M.
Hockaday, Joseph W.
Howes, David.
Hue, Constant L.
Hughes, James H.
Hudgel, Rezin D.
Hulburd, Loyal P.
Hurd, Orin D.

Jones, Maurice L.

Kieth, Robert F.
Knight, William.

Law, Charles D.
Liebman, Ernest F.
Lipsett, William E.
Loesch, George H.
Lorton, Jesse G.

McClure, John H.
McCracken, James K.
McDonald, Ranald T.
McKay, David.
Mahurin, Marshall S.
Manchester, Alfred E.
Markey, Andrew J.
Mauk, Frances M.
Metzner, Jasper.
Mordhurst, Henry W.
Morris, William P.
Moses, Frank D.
Munson, Charles A.

Nickey, Addison B.

Oakley, Chauncey B.
Olds, John D.
Orff, Charles E.
Orrock, William W.

Palmer, Earl.
Polhamus, Andrew H.

Pond, Olen J.
Probasco, William J.

Read, Charles E.
Reiter, George.
Rockhill, William W.
Ross, Edward C.
Ross, John.

Sauers, James T.
Scott, Harry K.
Sessford, Charles W.
Shambaugh, William H.
Simonson, James H.
Smick, Manford M.
Smith, Willard P.
Spencer, George W.
Staub, Alexander H.
Stemen, Christian B.
Stemen, George C.
Stouder, Frank E.
Study, Justin N.
Sweet, Samuel B.

Tapp, Herman W.
Taylor, Benjamin F.
Teagarden, Marion.
Thompson, Frank.
Tilio, Charles D.
Townsend, Dick.
Turner, Harvey K.

Umstead, Hiram D.

Vesey, William J.

Wales, Edward A.
Wallace, John.
White, John 1.
Wilding, Charles A.
Wilkens, Christian.
Williams, James B.
Wing, John F.
Wise, Aaron F.
(Died April 30, 1898.)

Zollars, Allen.

56

SCOTTISH RITE.

Colors All colors are used.

Calendar THE SCOTCH RITE, or SCOTTISH RITE OF FREEMASONRY, dates
the same as Ancient Craft Masonry, except the Jewish chronology is
used. *Anno-Mundi* (A. M.), meaning "In the Year of the World."
A. D. 1898—A. M. 5658.

ANCIENT ACCEPTED SCOTTISH RITE,
VALLEY OF FORT WAYNE.
FORT WAYNE LODGE OF PERFECTION.

Chartered September 19th, 1888.

WILLIAM GEAKE.

Thrice Potent Grand Master, from Date of Organization to Present
Time, June 1st, 1898.

Stated Meetings First and Third Tuesdays in each month.

Members designated "C. M." are charter members.

LIST OF MEMBERS.

Adair, Joseph W.	Columbia City.
Ahern, John E.	Pittsburgh, Pa.
Alden, Samuel R.	Fort Wayne.
Altevoght, Henry F.	"
Alstadler, Albert	Huntington.
Allen, George H.	Fort Wayne.
Allen, Richard	"
Allison, Robert B. C. M.	Decatur.
Andrews, J. Eugene	Garrett.
Archer, Charles E.	Fort Wayne.
Armstrong, James A.	"
Arnold, Daniel	Montpelier.
Arthur, James A.	Goshen.
Astry, Jonas	Fort Wayne.
Baker, Jeremiah	Garrett.
Baldwin, Merchant H.	Fort Wayne.
Barden, William N.	"
Barnett, Abraham G.	"
Barnett, James W.	"
Barr, Robert P.	Kendallville.
Barrett, James M.	Fort Wayne
Barthold, Frederick L.	"
Bash, Daniel F.	
Bash, Harry E.	"
Bash, Winfield S.	"
Bass, John H.	"
Bauer, John J.	"
Beatty, Frank M.	Ossian.
Beckley, Albert	Butler.
Beers, George W.	Fort Wayne.
Bell, Joseph W. C. M.	"
Bell, Benjamin F.	Bellevue, Ohio.
Belott, George E.	Fort Wayne.
Bennett, James R.	Bluffton.
Beyerle, Lincoln H.	Goshen.
Birget, Cyrus J.	Topeka, Kansas.
Bisel, Elmer E.	Fort Wayne.
Blakesley, Lyman M.	Olathe, Kansas.
Blitz, Maximillian J.	Fort Wayne.
Boehlen, Frederick	"
Bogue, Oliver H.	Wabash.
Boltz, Ferdinand F. C. M.	Bluffton.
Bond, Charles E.	Fort Wayne.
Bond, Charles Z.	"
Boughton, Henry C.	Ashland, Ky.

58

Bowser, Augustus	Fort Wayne.
Brant, Selwyn O.	Evansville.
Brillhart, Samuel B.	Kendallville.
Brokaw, James H.	Fort Wayne.
Bronson, John L.	LaFayette.
Brown, Edward F.	Andrews.
Brown, William L.	Mentone.
Brown, Isaac H.	Covington, Ky.
Buchman, Alpheus P.	Fort Wayne.
Budd, Francis F.	Utica, N. Y.
Bulson, Albert E.	Fort Wayne.
Burley, John H.	San Luis Potosi, Mexico.
Burnison, Daniel C.	Fostoria, Ohio.
Burrowes, Stephen A.	Fort Wayne.
Carruth, David E.	Auburn.
Case, Clinton M.	Kendallville.
Chadwick, John M.	Louisville, Ky.
Chandler, Oren J.	Warsaw.
Chapler, Martin L.	Wabash.
Clark, Frank H.	Montpelier.
Clark, Franklin	Toledo.
Clark, Jacob W.	Fort Wayne.
Clark, Joseph	Columbia City.
Clugston, Asher R.	"
Clugston, David B.	"
Clugston, William A.	"
Cohen, Henry	Fort Wayne.
Colson, Wiley M.	Toledo, Ohio.
Cook, Ernest W.	Fort Wayne.
Cook, Newton E.	Wellington, Kan.
Copenhaver Harry L.	Garrett.
Cotter, Bartlett E.	Providence, R. I.
Courtier, George S.	Wabash.
Cowen, Milliard R.	Fort Wayne.
Cowgill, Cary E.	Wabash.
Craig, James C.	Fort Wayne.
Cratsley, Frank C.	"
Craw, Edward L.	"
Creighton William	"
Cressler, Alfred D. C. M.	"
Cunison, James	"
Curtner John M.	Wabash.
Current, William A.	Fort Wayne.
Cutler, Albert H.	Covington, Ky.
Dailey, Eph P.	Fort Wayne.
Dalman, John	"

Danes, William S.	Peru.
Davenport, Lewis C. C. M.	Bluffton.
Davis, John L.	Auburn.
Dawson, Charles M.	Fort Wayne.
DePuy, Frank	Wabash.
Derr, Elmer E.	Ossian.
Detzer, Gustave G.	Fort Wayne.
Dickson, James M.	Peru.
Doty, Richard E.	Fort Wayne.
Donivan, John W.	"
Doud, Wallace E.	"
Dougall, John T.	Fort Wayne.
Doughman, Newton D.	"
Douglass, Robert F.	"
Downing, Myron	"
Drake, Thomas F.	"
Durfee, George A.	"
Eckert, David S.	"
Edington, Samuel C.	Poneto.
Edmunds, Frank W.	Fort Wayne.
Egbert, Hanes	Goshen.
Egbert, John W.	"
Elder, John M.	Chicago, Ohio.
Ellenwood, Horace D.	Poe.
Emrick, Emmett V.	Fort Wayne.
Emerick, Judson B.	Poe.
Ensleu, William	Fort Wayne.
Ettinger, George D.	Bourbon.
Evans, George P.	Fort Wayne.
Evans, Oscar	Chattanooga, Tenn
Everett, Charles E.	Fort Wayne.
Ewing, George W.	"
Fay, Monford W.	"
Fee, Frank F.	"
Feebleman, Joseph L.	Indianapolis.
Felts, George F.	Fort Wayne.
Fidler, William H.	New Waverly.
Fielde, William S.	Chicago, Ill.
Firestone, Allison D.	Columbia City.
Fisher, Francis M.	Battle Creek, Mich
Fister, George H.	Elkhart.
Fitch, Charles B.	Fort Wayne.
Ford, James H.	Wabash.
Ford, Samuel I.	Helena, Ohio.
Forgy, Dickinson J.	New Waverly.

Fowler, William . . .	Wabash.
Frederichs. William J. . .	Garrett.
Gale, George A.	Fort Wayne.
Gandy, Oscar	Churubusco.
Gardner, DeMotte C.	Fort Wayne.
Garman, John W.	"
Garrison, Kenton	Converse.
Garwood, Don A.	Auburn.
Gatchell, Ulyses G.	Upper Sandusky, O.
Gates, William F.	Peru.
Gauntt, Adin W.	Richmond.
Geake, William C. M. . . .	Fort Wayne.
Gibson, Jordan E.	Logansport.
Gillie, James	Fort Wayne.
Ginty, Michael O.	"
Glenn, John S.	Huntington.
Glenn, William M.	Fort Wayne.
Godfrey, George L.	"
Goodall, James B.	Peru.
Goodwin, Thomas A.	Warsaw.
Goodman, William	Fort Wayne.
Gould, Emmett A.	Peru.
Graham, James A.	Fort Wayne.
Granger, Horace G.	"
Gray, James P.	"
Greenewalt, George L. . . .	"
Greer, Thomas, Jr.	"
Greer, Thomas, Sr.	"
Griffin, Frank P.	Bourbon.
Griffith, James M.	Fort Wayne.
Griffith, Levi	"
Griffith, Morris E.	Baldwin.
Grindle, Alfred	Fort Wayne.
Griswold, Crawford	"
Grout, William H.	"
Gruber, Joseph L. C. M . . .	"
Gumpper, Jacob D.	"
Guynn, Lincoln	Wabash.
Hale, James P.	Bluffton.
Halderman, Louis	Larwill.
Halderman, Jacob	Fort Wayne.
Haller, John B.	Andrews.
Hanna, Henry C.	Fort Wayne.
Hanna, J. Thomas	"
Hanna, Joseph T.	"

Hanna, Robert B.	. . . . .	Fort Wayne.
Hanna, Samuel D.	. . . . .	"
Harding, Daniel L.	. . . . .	"
Harper, Benjamin F.	. . . . .	"
Harper, James B.	. . . . .	"
Harsh, George	. . . . .	"
Hatfield, James C.	. . . . .	Ossian.
Hattersley, Alfred C. M.	. . . . .	Fort Wayne.
Hattersley, Willis	. . . . .	"
Havice, Samuel H.	. . . . .	"
Hayden, John W.	. . . . .	"
Hazzard, Albert W.	. . . . .	"
Heath, Wilbur F.	. . . . .	Danville, Ills.
Heaton, Owen N.	. . . . .	Fort Wayne.
Hebert, Oliver	. . . . .	"
Heffley, Charles O.	. . . . .	Logansport.
Heit, Anthony W.	. . . . .	Fort Wayne.
Hendee, John C.	. . . . .	Garrett.
Henry, James M.	. . . . .	Fort Wayne.
Henry, John C.	. . . . .	South Whitley.
Higgins, Cecilius R.	. . . . .	Fort Wayne.
Hile, Frederick	. . . . .	"
Hilgeman, Henry F.	. . . . .	"
Hilton, Charles S.	. . . . .	"
Hiner, John M.	. . . . .	Peru.
Hoffman, G. Max	. . . . .	Fort Wayne.
Hoham, Frederick D.	. . . . .	"
Holmes, Abiram T.	. . . . .	"
Hosmer, Robert W.	. . . . .	Detroit. Mich.
Howard, Louis L.	. . . . .	Montpelier.
Howe, Maurice S.	. . . . .	Wabash.
Hue, Constant L.	. . . . .	Silverton, Colo.
Huffman, Cornelius H.	. . . . .	Danville, Ills.
Hughes, William M.	. . . . .	Columbia City.
Hull, Sylvester W.	. . . . .	Fort Wayne.
Humphrey, John C. M.	. . . . .	Indianapolis.
Died April 29, 1898.		
Humrichouser, Harry	. .	Pierceton.
Jackson, Appleton R.	. . . . .	Churubusco.
Jamieson, John E.	. . . . .	Peru.
Johnson, John M.	. . . . .	Warsaw.
Jones, Charles H. G.	. . . . .	Auburn.
Jones, Maurice L.	. . . . .	Fort Wayne.
Keeler, Joseph W.	. . . . .	"
Keeran, William H.	. . . . .	"

Kendrick, Charles E.	Fort Wayne.
Kenerk, Edward A.	"
Keppel, Charles H.	New Albany.
Kerr, Louis	Ligonier.
Kerr, Robert D.	"
Kerr, William W.	Fort Wayne.
Kerns, Theodore S.	Logansport.
Kesler, Abraham J.	Fort Wayne.
Kikley, Isadore P.	"
Kidd, John	"
King, Frank E.	"
King, William L.	Richmond.
Kircher, Frank M.	Garrett.
Xirk, Charles C.	Huntington.
Kleder, George M.	Milford.
Klingensmith, Jefferson C.	Montpelier.
Knapp, Jasper W.	Hinton, W. Va.
Knapp, William B.	Portland, Oregon.
Knight, Charles S.	Fort Wayne.
Knight, William	"
Knight, Lucellus G.	Montpelier.
Kuhne, Charles W.	Fort Wayne.
Kuhne, H. Richard	"
Lautz, James H.	Garrett.
Lantz, Reuben	"
Larimer, Joseph H.	Peru.
Latchem, John B.	Wabash.
Law, Charles D.	Fort Wayne.
Law, Herbert J.	"
Lawrence, George W.	Columbia City.
Leas, William H.	Waterloo.
Lee, Thomas B.	Bourbon.
Lenheim, Ulysses L. C. M.	Saginaw City, Mich.
Leonard, James H.	Pittsburgh, Pa.
Liebman, Ernest F.	Fort Wayne.
Ligget, Robert A.	"
Liggett, William H.	Columbia City.
Lipsett, William E.	Fort Wayne.
Liscum, James R.	Chillicothe, Ills.
Little, Martin W.	Huntington.
Loesch, George H.	Fort Wayne.
Lomas, Charles	West Superior, Wis
Lomas, Edward	Chicago, Ills.
Lones, Jerome H.	Warsaw.
Long, Lissel	Andrews.
Lorton, Jesse G.	Fort Wayne.

63

Lowe, George W.	Fort Wayne.
Lumbard, Sidney C.	"
Lysinger, George P.	Gas City.
McCausland, John W.	Fort Wayne.
McClintock, William B.	Peru.
McClure, John H.	Toledo, Ohio.
McCray, Elmer E. .	Kendallville.
McCracken, James K.	Fort Wayne.
McCulloch, Charles .	"
McCulloch, William O.	Warsaw.
McDonald, Ranald T. C. M.	Fort Wayne.
McFerran, S. Milton	"
McGuire, J. Howe .	Wabash.
McIlvaine, Thomas O.	Huntington.
McLallen, Elisha L., Jr.	Columbia City.
McLallen, Walter F.	"
McKay, David	Fort Wayne.
McKean, John L	"
McNutt, Willard C.	"
McPherson, Angus	"
Magley, William H. .	Columbia City.
Mahurin, Marshall S.	Fort Wayne.
Marshall, Thomas R.	Columbia City.
Mason, William D.	Bluffton.
Mathews, Frederick	Ellettsville.
Mathews, Oliver H. .	Chicago, Ills.
Mathews, William N.	Bedford.
Mauk, Francis M.	Fort Wayne.
Mayer, Thomas	Logansport.
Merriett, Charles F.	Fort Wayne.
Merryman, James T.	Decatur.
Metzner, Jasper	Fort Wayne.
Miesse, Harry	Grand Rapids, Mich
Miller, Albert F.	Valparaiso.
Miller, James E	Fort Wayne.
Miller, George F.	South Whitley.
Miles, LeRoy .	Milford.
Miles, William	Fort Wayne.
Mitchell, John	Kendallville.
Moore, George W.	Fort Wayne.
Moore, Samuel C.	"
Mordhurst, Henry W.	"
Morgan, Joseph D.	Dixon, Ohio.
Morris, John, Jr.	Fort Wayne.
Morris, William P.	"

Morrison, Walter S.	Huntington.
Morrison, William L.	Elkhart.
Moses, Frank D. . r .	St. Joseph, Mo.
Mossiman, Emanuel E. .	Bluffton.
Mossman, William E.	Fort Wayne.
Mulvey, Charles B. .	Montpelier
Munson, Charles A. (C. M.)	Fort Wayne.
Needham, Edward F. . .	"
Newman, Miles N.	Ossian.
Nickey, Addison B.	Princeton.
Nickey, Samuel M.	"
North, George W.	Columbia City.
North, Jere . .	Bluffton.
Nye, Charles F. .	Warsaw.
Oakley, Chauncey B. C. M.)	Fort Wayne.
Oglesbee, Rollo B. . .	Plymouth.
Olds, John D. . .	Fort Wayne.
O'Neal, Oren .	Chicago, Ills.
Oppenheim, Albert . .	Bluffton.
Orff, Charles E.	Fort Wayne.
O'Rourke, Edward	"
Orr, John W. .	"
Parks, Harry I.	Kendallville.
Peabody, James B.	Los Angeles, Cal.
Penman, Robert P.	Fort Wayne.
Penrod, John W. .	Goshen.
Perrine, Van B. .	Fort Wayne.
Peterson, John S. .	Decatur.
Phelps, William H. . . .	Fort Wayne.
Pixley, George W. C. M. . .	"
Pond, Olen J. . . .	New Haven.
Porter, Miles F. .	Fort Wayne.
Powers, Frank M.	Angola.
Probasco, William J.	Fort Wayne.
Pullman, Bernard	Kendallville.
Quick, Lowry L.	New Waverly.
Quick, Otho L.	"
Rabus, George	Fort Wayne.
Randall, Perry A.	"
Randall, Sumner K.	Avilla.
Read, Charles E. .	Fort Wayne.
Rehorst, Frederick .	"
Reef, Nashau G. . .	Albion.
Reinking, Frederick W. ,	Fort Wayne.

Reiter, George	Fort Wayne.
Reynolds, Homer B.	"
Richardson, Benjamin F.	Warsaw.
Richason, George B.	Delphos, Ohio.
Richason, William M.	Peru.
Rider, Frank A.	Fort Wayne.
Roberts, George I.	"
Robertson, Robert S.	"
Robertson, Walter A.	"
Robeson, William C.	Montpelier.
Robinson, Amassa S.	Monroeville.
Robinson, James M.	Fort Wayne.
Rockhill, William W. C. M.	"
Rogers, James C. M.	"
Romy, Robert L.	"
Roscoe, James	Albion.
Rose, Haswell D.	Fort Wayne,
Ross, Edward C.	Eagle Lake.
Ross, George A.	Fort Wayne.
Ross, John	"
Ross, John E.	"
Rossington, Rodolphus B.	"
Rowe, John A.	Frankfort.
Rowland, Harry W.	Franklin.
Rurode, Ernest C.	Fort Wayne.
Rutter, Richard S.	Warsaw.
Sargent, Theodore C.	LaFayette.
Sauer, Carl	Fort Wayne,
Sauers, James T.	"
Sawyer, Frederick E.	"
Sayre, George B.	Mansfield, Ohio.
Schilling, Carl,	Fort Wayne.
Scott, Harry K.	Angola.
Scott, William H.	Barnesville, Minn.
Seibold, Julius	Peru.
Shambaugh, William H.	Fort Wayne.
Sharp, James H.	Columbia City.
Sheffield, George S.	Chicago, Ills.
Shumaker, Samuel F.	Norfolk, Va.
Sine, Amos	Fort Wayne.
Siver, Emett L.	"
Skiles, Harmon T.	Bluffton.
Slack, James R.	Huntington.
Smith, Eugene B.	Fort Wayne.
Smith, Henry I.	"
Smith, Reader P.	"

66

Snavelley, William K.	Wabash.
Spencer, Milton E.	Ossian.
Spielman, John A.	Garrett.
Sprague, Harry E.	Fort Wayne.
Stahl, Charles F.	"
Staub, Alexander H.	"
Stephan, Wilhelm F.	"
Sterling, Reynolds	"
Stemen, Christian B. C. M.	"
Stemen, George C.	"
Stemen, William E.	Kansas City, Kas.
Stevens, Frederick M.	Bluffton.
Stevens, John S.	Los Angeles, Cal.
Sties, John E.	Chicago, Ills.
Stilson, George W.	Fort Wayne.
Stouder, Frank E.	
Strong, Eph K.	Columbia City.
Study, Justin N.	Fort Wayne.
Sunderland, Joseph E.	"
Sutter, J. R.	Kansas City, Mo.
Swart, George W.	Huntington.
Sweringen, Budd V.	Fort Wayne.
Sweringen, Frank H.	"
Sweet, Samuel B. C. M.	Indianapolis.
Swick, Peter D.	Roanoke.
Swindell, Charles H.	Plymouth
Talmage, Charles H.	Indianapolis.
Tapp, Ferdinand	Fort Wayne.
Tapp, Herman W.	"
Teagarden, Harvey J.	Springfield, Ohio.
Teagarden, Marion	Fort Wayne.
Telley, George W.	"
Thayer, James W.	Plymouth.
Thieme, John A.	Fort Wayne.
Thompson, Benjamin F.	"
Thompson, Richard G.	"
Tibbles, Frank E.	"
Tillo, Charles D.	"
Titus, Charles H.	"
Todd, Jacob J. C. M.	Bluffton.
Todd, Warner M	Fort Wayne.
Townsend, Dick	Decatur.
Tucker, Frederick W.	Warsaw.
Turner, Harvey K.	Fort Wayne.
Tuttle, Caldwell W.	Columbia City.
Umstead, Hiram D.	Fort Wayne.

Vallette, William O.	Goshen.
Vance, John C.	Logansport.
Vesey, William J.	Fort Wayne.
Vordermark, John W.	"
Walter, Amos R.	"
Walter, Harry H.	"
Warner, Cyrene	Bluffton.
Watt, William H.	New York, N. Y.
Weaver, Levi B.	Warsaw.
Webb, Isaiah D	"
Webster, Benjamin H.	Nine Mile.
Welbaum, John L.	"
Wenger, Noah R.	Fort Wayne.
Wheelock, Kent K.	"
Wherry, William P.	"
White, R. Parks	Warsaw.
Whitesett, Robert B.	Logansport.
Wilding, Charles A.	Fort Wayne.
Wilding, James W. Died April 7, 1898.	"
Wilkens, Christian	"
Wilkens, Jacob V.	"
Williams, Frank E.	Wabash.
Williams, James B.	Fort Wayne.
Wilson, Frank W.	Forrest, Ills.
Wilson, George W.	Fort Wayne.
Wilson, Lamley F.	Ossian.
Wilson, Solomon	Wabash.
Wilt, Frank P.	Fort Wayne.
Wing, John F. C. M.	"
Wood, Israel O.	Goshen.
Wood, Frank J.	Warsaw.
Wood, J. Fordyce	Washington, D C.
Wood, Paul E.	Fort Wayne.
Wyman, Albert H.	Huntington.
Yarnelle, William R.	Wabash.
Zollars, Allen C. M.	Fort Wayne.
Zollinger, Henry C.	"

Henry W. Mordhurst

DARIUS COUNCIL, PRINCES OF JERUSALEM.

Chartered April 9th, 1889.

PAST SOV. GRAND MASTERS.

HENRY W. MORDHURST...1889-1890.
CHARLES M. DAWSON..1890 to 1896.
HENRY W. MORDHURST...1896 to 1898.

Stated Meetings Second and Fourth Tuesdays in each month.

Members designated " C. M." are charter members.

LIST OF MEMBERS.

Adair, Joseph W.	Columbia City.
Ahern, John E.	Pittsburgh, Pa.
Alden, Samuel R.	Fort Wayne.
Altevoght, Henry F.	"
Alstadler, Albert	Huntington.
Allen, George H.	Fort Wayne.
Allen, Richard	"
Allison, Robert B.	Decatur.
Andrews, J. Eugene	Garrett.
Archer, Charles E.	Fort Wayne.
Armstrong, James A.	"
Arnold, Daniel	Montpelier.
Arthur, James A.	Goshen.
Baker, Jeremiah	Garrett.
Barden, William N.	Fort Wayne.
Barnett, Abraham G.	"
Barnett, James W.	"
Barrett, James M.	"
Bash, Daniel F.	"
Bass, John H. C. M.	"
Bauer, John J.	"

Beckley, Albert	Butler.
Beers, George W.	Fort Wayne.
Bell, Joseph W. (C. M.)	"
Bell, Benjamin F.	Bellevue, Ohio.
Belott, George E.	Fort Wayne.
Beyerle, Lincoln H.	Goshen.
Blakesley, Lyman M.	Olathe, Kansas
Blitz, Maximillian J.	Fort Wayne.
Boehlen, Frederick	"
Bogue, Oliver H.	Wabash.
Boltz, Ferdinand F. (C. M.)	Bluffton.
Bond, Charles E.	Fort Wayne.
Bowser, Augustus	Fort Wayne.
Bronson, John L.	LaFayette.
Brown, Edward F.	Andrews.
Brown, William L.	Mentone.
Brown, Isaac H.	Covington, Ky.
Buchman, Alpheus P.	Fort Wayne.
Budd, Francis F.	Utica, N. Y.
Bulson, Albert E.	Fort Wayne.
Burrowes, Stephen A.	"
Carruth, David E.	Auburn.
Case, Clinton M.	Kendallville.
Chadwick, John M.	Louisville, Ky.
Chandler, Oren J.	Warsaw.
Chapler, Martin L.	Wabash.
Clark, Frank H.	Montpelier.
Clark, Jacob W.	Fort Wayne.
Clugston, Asher R.	Columbia City.
Clugston, William A.	"
Cook, Ernest W.	Fort Wayne.
Copenhaver, Harry L.	Garrett.
Cotter, Bartlett E.	Providence, R. I.
Courtier, George S.	Wabash.
Cowgill, Cary E.	"
Craig, James C.	Fort Wayne.
Cressler, Alfred D.	"
Curtner, John M.	Wabash.
Current, William A.	Fort Wayne.
Cutler, Albert H.	Covington, Ky.
Dailey, Eph P.	Fort Wayne.
Dalman, John	"
Danes, William S.	Peru.
Davenport, Lewis C. (C. M.)	Bluffton.
Davis, John L.	Auburn.
Dawson, Charles M. (C. M.)	Fort Wayne.

DePuy, Frank	Wabash.
Detzer, Gustave G.	Fort Wayne.
Donivan, John W.	"
Doud, Wallace E.	"
Dougall, John T.	"
Doughman, Newton D.	"
Douglass, Robert F.	"
Durfee, George A.	"
Eckert, David S.	"
Edington, Samuel C.	Poneto.
Edmunds, Frank W.	Fort Wayne.
Egbert, Hanes	Goshen.
Egbert, John W.	"
Elder, John M. . . . . . . ♥	Chicago, Ohio.
Ellenwood, Horace D.	Poe.
Emerick, Judson B.	Poe.
Emrick, Emmett V.	Fort Wayne.
Evans, George P.	Fort Wayne.
Evans, Oscar	Chattanooga, Tenn
Everett, Charles E.	Fort Wayne.
Ewing, George W.	"
Fay, Monford W.	"
Fee, Frank F.	"
Feebleman, Joseph L.	Indianapolis.
Felts, George F.	Fort Wayne.
Fidler, William H.	New Waverly.
Fielde, William S.	Chicago, Ill.
Fisher, Francis M.	Battle Creek, Mich
Fisher, George H.	Elkhart.
Fitch, Charles B.	Fort Wayne.
Ford, James H.	Wabash.
Ford, Samuel I.	Helena, Ohio.
Forgy, Dickinson J.	New Waverly.
Fowler, William	Wabash.
Frederichs, William J.	Garrett.
Gale, George A.	Fort Wayne.
Gandy, Oscar	Churubusco.
Gardner, DeMotte C. 'C. M.' . . .	Fort Wayne.
Garrison, Kenton	Converse.
Garwood, Don A.	Auburn.
Gates, William F.	Peru.
Gauntt, Adin W.	Richmond.
Geake, William 'C. M.'	Fort Wayne.
Gillie, James	"
Glenn, John S.	Huntington.

71

Glenn, William M. C. M.	Fort Wayne.
Godfrey, George L. C. M.	"
Goodall, James B.	Peru.
Goodwin, Thomas A.	Warsaw.
Goodman, William	Fort Wayne.
Gould, Emmett A.	Peru.
Graham, James A.	Fort Wayne.
Granger, Horace G.	"
Gray, James P. C. M.	"
Greenawalt, George L.	"
Greer, Thomas, Jr.	"
Griffin, Frank P.	Bourbon.
Griffith, Levi C. M.	Fort Wayne.
Griffith, Morris E.	Baldwin.
Grindle, Alfred	Fort Wayne.
Griswold, Crawford	"
Grout, William H.	"
Gruber, Ioseph L. C. M.	"
Guynn, Lincoln	Wabash.
Halderman, Lonis	Larwill.
Halderman, Jacob	Fort Wayne.
Haller, John B.	Andrews.
Hanna, Henry C. C. M.	Fort Wayne.
Harding, Daniel L.	"
Harper, Benjamin F.	"
Harper, James B.	"
Harsh, George	"
Hattersley, Alfred C. M.)	"
Hattersley, Willis	"
Havice, Samuel H.	"
Hayden, John W. C. M.)	"
Hazzard, Albert W.	"
Heath, Wilbur F. C. M.	Danville, Ills.
Heaton, Owen N.	Fort Wayne.
Hebert, Oliver	"
Hendee, John C.	Garrett.
Henry, James M.	Fort Wayne.
Henry, John C.	South Whitley.
Higgins, Cecilius R.	Fort Wayne.
Hile, Frederick	"
Hilgeman, Henry F.	"
Hilton, Charles S.	"
Hiner, John M.	Peru.
Hoffman, G. Max	Fort Wayne.
Hosmer, Robert W.	Detroit, Mich.
Howard, Louis L.	Montpelier.

72

Howe, Maurice S.	Wabash.
Hue, Constant L.	Silverton, Colo.
Huffman, Cornelius H.	Danville, Ills.
Humphrey, John C. M.	Indianapolis.
Died April 29, 1898.	
Humrichouser, Harry	Pierceton.
Jamieson, John E.	Peru.
Jones, Charles H. G.	Auburn.
Jones, Maurice L.	Fort Wayne.
Kendrick, Charles E.	"
Kerr, Louis	Ligonier.
Kerr, William W.	Fort Wayne.
Kikley, Isadore P.	"
Kidd, John	"
King, Frank E.	"
King, William L.	Richmond.
Kircher, Frank M.	Garrett.
Kirk, Charles C.	Huntington.
Kleder, George M.	Milford.
Klingensmith, Jefferson C.	Montpelier.
Knapp, William B.	Portland, Oregon.
Knight, Charles S.	Fort Wayne.
Knight, Lucullus G.	Montpelier.
Kuhne, Charles W.	Fort Wayne.
Lantz, James H.	Garrett.
Lantz, Reuben	"
Larimer, Joseph H.	Peru.
Latchem, John B.	Wabash.
Law, Charles D.	Fort Wayne.
Lawrence, George W.	Columbia City.
Leas, William H.	Waterloo.
Lee, Thomas B.	Bourbon.
Leonard, James H.	Pittsburgh, Pa.
Liebman, Ernest F.	Fort Wayne.
Ligget, Robert A.	"
Lipsett, William E.	"
Loesch, George H.	"
Lones, Jerome H.	Warsaw.
Long, Lissel	Andrews.
Lumbard, Sidney C.	Fort Wayne.
McCausland, John W.	"
McClure, John H.	Andrews.
McCracken, James K.	Fort Wayne.
McCray, Elmer E.	Kendallville.

73

McCulloch, Charles	Fort Wayne.
McDonald, Ranald T.	"
McFerran, S. Milton	"
McGuire, J. Howe	Wabash.
McLallen, Elisha L., Jr.	Columbia City.
McLallen, Walter F.	"
McKay, David	Fort Wayne.
McKean, John L	"
McNutt, Willard C.	"
Magley, William H.	Columbia City.
Mahurin, Marshall S. C. M.	Fort Wayne.
Marshall, Thomas R. C. M.	Columbia City.
Mathews, Frederick	Ellettsville.
Mathews, Oliver H.	Chicago, Ills.
Mathews, William N.	Bedford.
Mauk, Francis M.	Fort Wayne.
Merryman, James T.	Decatur.
Metzner, Jasper	Fort Wayne.
Meyer, Thomas C. M.	Logansport.
Miesse, Harry	Grand Rapids, Mich
Miller, James E	Fort Wayne.
Miller, George F.	South Whitley.
Miles, LeRoy	Milford.
Miles, William	Fort Wayne.
Mitchell, John	Kendallville.
Moore, George W. C. M.	Fort Wayne.
Moore, Samuel C.	"
Mordhurst, Henry W. C. M.	"
Morgan, Joseph D.	Dixon, Ohio.
Morris, John, Jr.	Fort Wayne.
Morris, William P. C. M.	"
Morrison, Walter S.	Huntington.
Morrison, William L.	Elkhart.
Moses, Frank D. r	St. Joseph, Mo.
Mossiman, Emanuel E.	Bluffton.
Mossman, William E.	Fort Wayne.
Mulvey, Charles B.	Montpelier
Munson, Charles A. (C. M.)	Fort Wayne.
Needham, Edward F.	"
Newman, Miles N.	Ossian.
Nickey, Addison B.	Princeton.
Nickey, Samuel M.	"
North, George W.	Columbia City.
North, Jere	Bluffton.
Nye, Charles F.	Warsaw.

74

Oakley, Chauncey B.	Fort Wayne.
Oglesbee, Rollo B.	Plymouth.
Olds, John D. C. M.	Fort Wayne.
O'Neal, Oren .	Chicago, Ills.
Oppenheim, Albert .	Bluffton.
Orff, Charles E. C. M.	Fort Wayne.
O'Rourke, Edward	"
Peabody, James B.	Los Angeles, Cal.
Penman, Robert P.	Fort Wayne.
Penrod, John W.	Goshen.
Perrine, Van B. .	Fort Wayne.
Peterson, John S.	Decatur.
Phelps, William H. .	Fort Wayne.
Pixley, George W. C. M.	"
Pond, Olen J. .	New Haven.
Porter, Miles F. .	Fort Wayne.
Powers, Frank M.	Angola.
Probasco, William J.	Fort Wayne.
Pullman, Bernard	Kendallville.
Quick, Lowry L. .	New Waverly.
Quick, Otho L. . .	"
Rabus, George .	Fort Wayne.
Randall, Perry A. .	"
Randall, Sumner K. .	Avilla.
Read, Charles E. C. M.	Fort Wayne.
Rehorst, Frederick .	"
Reinking, Frederick W. ,	"
Reiter, George .	"
Reynolds, Homer B. .	"
Richardson, Benjamin F.	Warsaw.
Richason, George B. .	Delphos, Ohio.
Richason, William M.	Peru.
Robertson, Robert S.	Fort Wayne.
Robeson, William C.	Montpelier.
Robinson, James M.	Fort Wayne.
Robinson, Amassa S. .	Monroeville.
Rockhill, William W. C. M.	Fort Wayne.
Rogers, James	"
Romy, Robert L. .	"
Roscoe, James .	Albion.
Rose, Haswell D. .	Fort Wayne.
Ross, Edward C. .	Winona Lake.
Ross, George A. .	Fort Wayne.
Ross, John . .	"
Ross, John E.	"
Rossington, Rodolphus B.	"

Rowland, Harry W.	Franklin.
Rurode, Ernest C.	Fort Wayne.
Rutter, Richard S.	Warsaw.
Sargent, Theodore C.	LaFayette.
Sauer, Carl .	Fort Wayne,
Sawyer, Frederick E. .	"
Sayre, George B. . .	Mansfield, Ohio.
Schilling, Carl, . .	Fort Wayne.
Scott, Harry K. .	Angola.
Scott, William H. .	Barnesville, Minn.
Shambaugh, William H.	Fort Wayne.
Sheffield, George S. .	Chicago, Ills.
Shumaker, Samuel F. .	Norfolk, Va.
Siver, Emmet L. .	Fort Wayne.
Skiles, Harmon T. .	Bluffton.
Smith, Reader P. . .	Fort Wayne.
Snavelley, William K. .	Wabash.
Spielman, John A.	Garrett.
Sprague, Harry E.	Fort Wayne,
Stahl, Charles F.	"
Staub, Alexander H.	"
Stephan, Wilhelm .	"
Sterling, Reynolds . .	"
Stemen, Christian B. (C. M.)	"
Stemen, George C. . .	"
Stevens, Frederick M. .	Bluffton.
Stevens, John S. (C. M.) .	Los Angeles, Cal.
Stouder, Frank E. .	Fort Wayne.
Strong, Eph K. .	Columbia City.
Study, Justin N. .	Fort Wayne.
Sunderland, Joseph E.	"
Sutter, J. R. (C. M. .	Kansas City, Mo.
Swart, George W. .	Huntington.
Sweringen, Budd V.	Fort Wayne.
Sweringen, Frank H.	"
Sweet, Samuel P. (C. M.)	Indianapolis.
Swick, Peter D. .	Roanoke.
Swindell, Charles H.	Plymouth.
Talmage, Charles H.	Indianapolis.
Tapp, Ferdinand .	Fort Wayne.
Teagarden, Harvey J.	Springfield, Ohio.
Teagarden, Marion (C. M.)	Fort Wayne.
Thayer, James W. . .	Plymouth.
Thieme, John A. . .	Fort Wayne.
Thompson, Benjamin F. .	"
Thompson, Richard G. . .	"

76

Tibbles, Frank E.	Fort Wayne.
Tillo, Charles D.	"
Titus, Charles H.	"
Todd, Jacob J. C. M	Bluffton.
Todd, Warner M	Fort Wayne.
Townsend, Dick	Decatur.
Tucker, Frederick W.	Warsaw.
Turner, Harvey K.	Fort Wayne.
Tuttle, Caldwell W.	Columbia City.
Vallette, William O.	Goshen.
Vesey, William J.	Fort Wayne.
Vordermark, John W.	"
Walter, Amos R.	"
Walter, Harry II.	"
Watt, William II.	New York, N. Y
Weaver, Levi B.	Warsaw.
Webb, Isaiah D	"
Wenger, Noah R.	Fort Wayne.
Wheelock, Kent K.	"
Wherry, William P.	"
White, R. Parks	Warsaw.
Wilding, Charles A. C. M.	Fort Wayne.
Wilding, James W. Died April 7, 1898.	"
Wilkens, Jacob V.	"
Williams, Frank E.	Wabash.
Williams, James B. C. M.	Fort Wayne.
Wilson, Frank W.	Forrest, Ills.
Wilson, George W.	Fort Wayne.
Wilson, Solomon	Wabash.
Wilt, Frank P.	Fort Wayne.
Wing, John F. C. M.	"
Wood, Israel O.	Goshen.
Wood, Frank J.	Warsaw.
Wood, J. Fordyce	Washington, D C.
Wood, Paul E.	Fort Wayne.
Wyman, Albert H.	Huntington.
Yarnelle, William R.	Wabash.
Zollars, Allen C. M.	Fort Wayne.
Zollinger, Henry C.	"